Binding Crazy Angles

Mastering Curves, Points, Cleavage, and More
Ebony Love

Table of Contents

Introduction 5

Part 1: Binding Supplies 7
    Pins, Needles, Clips and Thread 7
    Marking and Measuring 9
    Sewing Machine 10
    Machine Presser Feet 11
    Binding Control 13

Part 2: Binding Basics 15
    Types of French-fold Binding 15
    Calculate the Binding Strip Width 16
    Calculate the Binding Length 17
    Determine the Fabric Required 18
    Prepare the Binding Fabric 19

Part 3: Make Bias Binding 23
    Cut Bias Binding Strips 23
    Sew Bias Binding Strips 26
    Press Binding Strips 28

Part 4: Prepare to Bind the Quilt 31
    Prep, Baste and Trim the Quilt 31
    Test Machine Settings 33

Part 5: Binding Wide Angles 39
    What is a Wide Angle? 39
    Getting Started with Wide Angles 39
    Mark the Wide Angle and Stitch the Binding .. 40
    Finish the Wide Angle Binding 44

Part 6: Binding Points ... 49
- What is a Point? ... 49
- Getting Started with Points ... 49
- Mark the Point and Stitch the Binding ... 49
- Finish the Pointed Binding ... 53

Part 7: Binding Curves ... 59
- Getting Started with Curves ... 59
- Stitch Curved Binding ... 59
- Finish the Curved Binding ... 60

Part 8: Binding Cleavage ... 63
- What is Cleavage? ... 63
- Getting Started with Cleavage ... 63
- Mark the Cleavage and Stitch the Binding ... 63
- Finish the Cleavage Binding ... 66

Part 9: Finish the Binding ... 73
- Connect the Binding Tails ... 73
- Finish the Machine Stitching ... 76

Part 10: Further Resources ... 79
- Where to Purchase ... 79
- Videos and Classes ... 80
- Frequently Asked Questions ... 81

Part i

Introduction

I'll never forget the disappointment on my students' faces when they showed up for machine binding class with angled-edge table runners, hoping I would help them finish their quilts.

"I'm sorry," I said. "If I have time I will try to help you, but I have to get everyone else started on their binding first."

It's very challenging in a short 3-hour class to cover everything someone might want to know about a set of techniques, but I always remembered those students and vowed to do something about it someday.

I'm so excited that "someday" has become now, and I hope after seeing the extensive lessons shared in this book, my students will understand why I wasn't able to switch gears into teaching a completely different technique that day.

Most of the complexity in binding crazy angles is pivoting in the right place and learning how to fold corners. Most of us have only been trained on 90° corners, but you'll find that they work the same way when you break down the technique.

This book does assume that you've already taken steps to give your quilts crazy angles; inside, for example, you won't find detailed instructions on how to scallop the edge of a quilt, but it does tell you how to bind a quilt you've already decided to scallop.

I hope this book brings you many days of trouble-free binding, knowing you can tackle any crazy angle that life's quilts throw at you!

Part 1: Binding Supplies

There are dozens of binding finishing techniques out there, with just as many people teaching these techniques and supplies to go with them. There are a few tools that I use almost all the time, and they are useful to have when binding quilts with unusual finishes. Check the Resources section for where to purchase.

Pins, Needles, Clips and Thread

The quality of what holds your quilts together, both temporarily and permanently, is so important to getting a neat finish for your binding.

Clover 1½" Patchwork Glasshead Pins

These extra-fine pins pass through fabric cleanly and don't cause additional bulk.

I love using these to help pin down points or secure folded corners until I can stitch them down by hand. Strategically placing pins is like having an extra pair of hands!

I also love these pins for securing binding that I intend to stitch by machine. Because the pins are so thin, you can stitch over them more safely than a bulkier pin. If you do hit one while stitching, you're more likely to bend or break the pin than the needle.

Binding Crazy Angles: Mastering Curves, Points, Cleavage, and More

Size 9 or 10 Quilting Needles (Betweens)

Quilting needles are shorter than other hand needles, which makes them more maneuverable for making nearly-invisible blind stitches.

In hand needle sizes, the larger the number, the smaller the needle. Size is a personal preference, but in general, I stitch binding by hand using a 10. You might find a 9 (or even an 8) more comfortable.

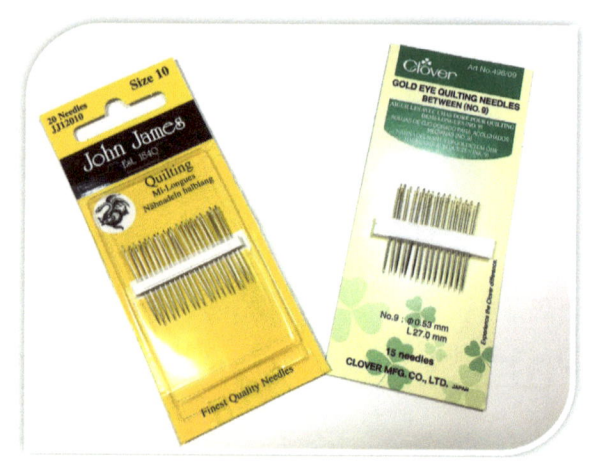

Aurifil 50wt Cotton Mako Thread

Use a neutral colored thread for basting and stitching the binding to the quilt.

To finish the binding, a matching thread is better to reduce the visibility of your stitching and blend into the binding fabric. A small 200m spool is usually sufficient to finish the binding on even a king-sized quilt.

Binding Clips

Binding clips are great for holding the binding in place for hand stitching, especially around curved edges.

They are a nice alternative to pins that won't prick you as you manipulate your project - and with crazy angles, you're always manipulating the project!

Clips can come in a variety of sizes; I prefer using the smallest size as they are more maneuverable in tight spaces.

Part 1: Binding Supplies

Marking and Measuring

With the right supplies, binding your quilts becomes almost a ritual. Marking and measuring accurately during the process keeps everything square and accurate.

Clover Chaco Liner Chalk

These fine-line chalk markers work great in combination with a straight line ruler, and dispense just the right amount of chalk.

Keep a light and dark chalk on hand for visibility on a variety of fabrics.

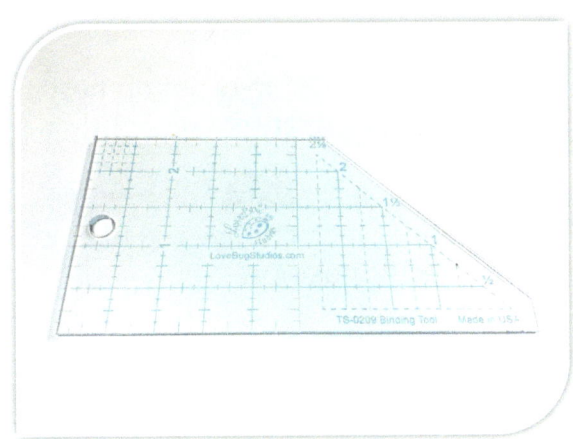

LoveBug Studios Binding Tool

The angled, dog-eared side helps for mitering strips and connecting the tails of the binding, while the square side aids in turning corners and measuring the overlap to finish stitching the binding to the quilt.

The long straight edge helps mark the seam allowance and to insure the proper angle is applied at corners.

There are many binding tools on the market, but most are focused on cutting the strips and mitering the seams. The tool I developed can be used throughout the process. It's small enough to keep at your machine, and the ⅛" markings along the ruler make it a versatile tool for marking and measuring. It can also be used as a braid template or to cut small half-square triangles from 2½" or smaller strips.

Binding Crazy Angles: Mastering Curves, Points, Cleavage, and More

Measuring Tape

If your quilt has a lot of twists and turns along the edge, traditional methods for calculating the binding might not work.

A flexible measuring tape can help you tackle these elusive measurements and help you understand how much binding you need to finish your project.

Sewing Machine

You don't need a top-of-the-line $10,000 sewing machine to get great results using these techniques. There are some features that will be helpful for you to have, and this will vary by the type of machine you are using.

Vintage or Industrial Machine

Many vintage and industrial machines are uniquely different from other domestic machines in that they are only capable of doing a single type of stitch: straight!

These machines will typically only have the ability to stitch forward and reverse, with an adjustable stitch length. However, you won't be able to change the needle position, or automatically stop with the needle in a specific position.

Can you still use the techniques here with one of these machines? Yes, but you will need to make accommodations for that equipment. Instead of being able to position the needle, you will have to mark guides on your throat plate.

Specialty feet may not be available, and you'd have to make accommodations for that too.

Since the binding will be finished by hand, there's no reason you couldn't use a vintage machine with these binding techniques.

Part 1: Binding Supplies

Modern or Domestic Sewing Machine

Modern (domestic) machines are capable of performing both straight stitches and at least a zigzag stitch. You'll be able to stitch forward and backward, and the needle will also be able to move side to side. Because of this, your machine may also have the ability to change the position of the needle over the throat plate.

If your machine has any or all of these additional features, you will have an easier time learning this technique and reproducing it regularly as detailed in this book:

- automatically stops with needle down;

- presser foot "hover" or knee lift - with needle down, presser foot can lift slightly to allow adjustments to the position of your project;

- quick change of presser feet and settings;

- adjustable stitch position – can shift a decorative stitch left or right to stitch in a different place;

- stitch memory – able to "save" favorite or commonly used stitches to recall later; and/or

- presser foot pressure or height adjustment – helps when stitching thicker materials.

Machine Presser Feet

With this technique, a couple of feet will come in very handy.

The good news is: you won't need a walking foot! You can certainly use one if you prefer, but I haven't needed to use one for any of these techniques.

Narrow Zipper Foot

This type of foot is great for more than just zippers. The narrow profile and length allow you to hold more of the quilt surface when basting the edges of the top to secure it to the batting and backing.

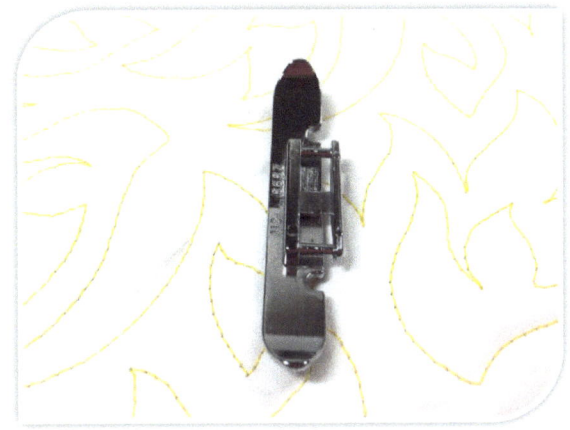

Binding Crazy Angles: Mastering Curves, Points, Cleavage, and More

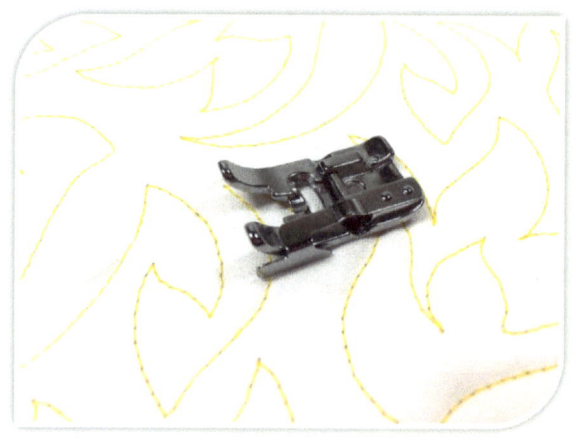

Edge Stitching Foot

This foot features a metal guide on the right side of the foot and a wide opening for adjusting the needle position. Place your fabric to the left of the guide, and adjust your needle to the correct position.

Some versions of this foot also allow adjustment of the outside guide. Avoid guides placed in the center of the foot.

A ¼" piecing foot is also helpful to have. However, if your Edge Stitching foot is able to accommodate the ¼", it's one less foot you need to keep track of.

What if specialty feet aren't available?

The narrow zipper foot is only for basting the edges of the quilt. Technically, you can do that with any foot, but I like the zipper foot because it rides along the edge and I don't have to think about it.

The edge guide foot (at least the one I have) can be set up for pretty much any needle position. I like the guide on the far right because the thickness of the quilt sandwich rides next to the guide, so my stitches are more accurately placed.

But if all you have is a regular foot, you can still do this! It just might mean slowing down and guiding your project more firmly. Your technique will improve with either practice, with better tools, or both. Just don't let the perfect get in the way of the good.

Part 1: Binding Supplies

Binding Control

These supplies aren't strictly required, but they do help with managing the binding throughout the process.

Binding Babies by Doohikey Designs

These are a fun and whimsical alternative to a simple cardboard tube or letting the binding puddle on the floor.

The medium and large sizes are the most common for quilt binding, and they come in a variety of colors and hair styles.

Dry Iron

This no-frills iron gets extremely hot, does not have an auto-shut off, and has a solid sole plate.

The solid sole plate and lack of moisture means no surprises with unexpected spots or debris falling onto the quilt or binding.

Stiletto

Sometimes binding needs a little more control, and putting your fingers too close to the needle can be a dangerous option.

Stilettos come in metal, wood, plastic, and all combinations in between. The best ones fit comfortably in your hand and keep you at a suitable distance from the needle. They also act like precision fingers to help you maneuver tight spaces!

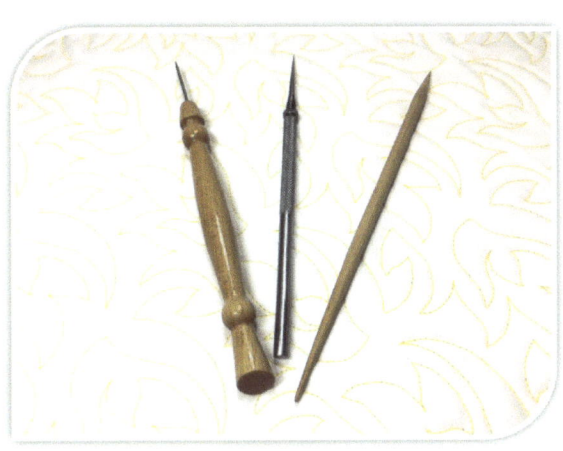

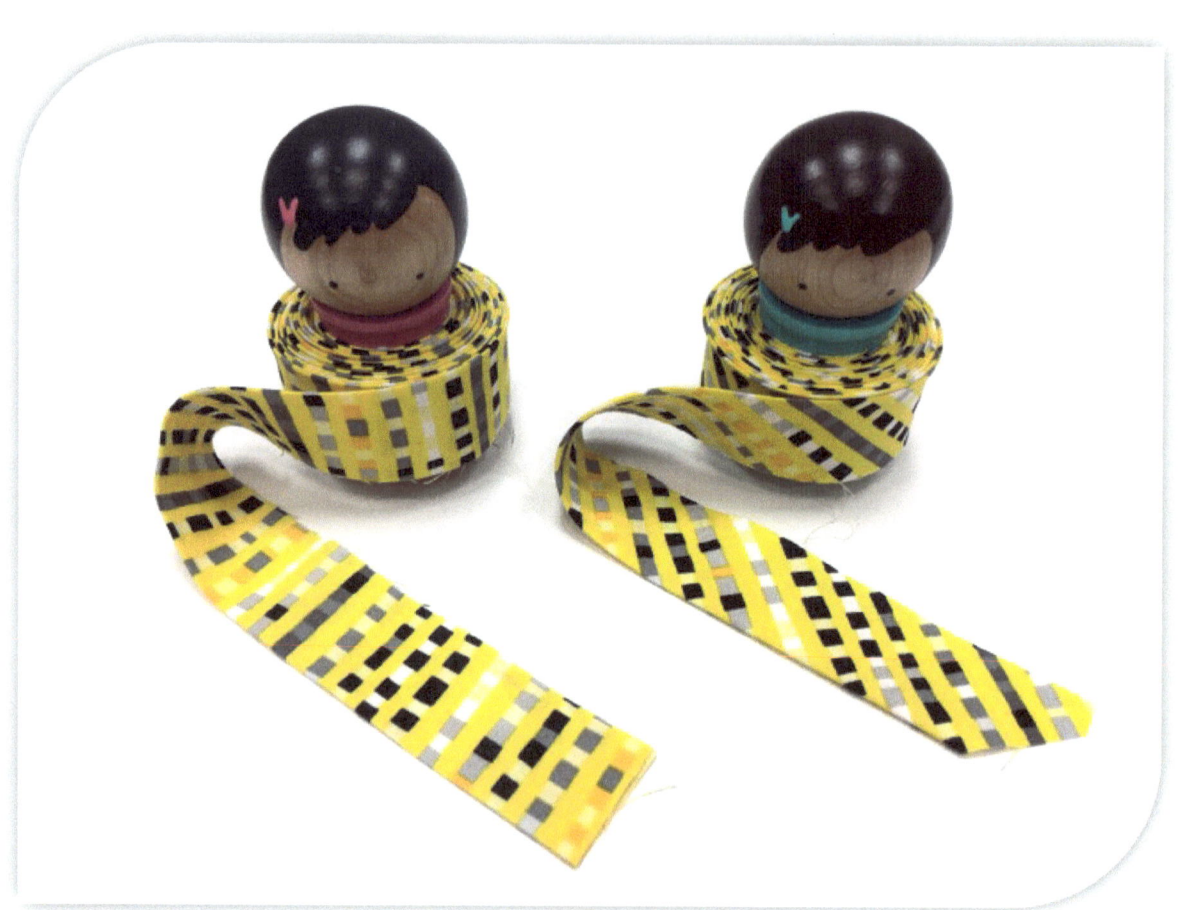

Part 2: Binding Basics

One of the first things I think about when working on my quilting projects is the method I want to use to bind my quilts. There are so many different ways to finish your quilts! You can face the edges, use single-fold binding, French-fold (double-fold) binding, turn the binding from the backing fabric, use prairie points — the possibilities are truly endless. We're going to focus on French-fold binding throughout the book; if you want to use single-fold binding instead, there are a few tips for modifying this method in *Part 8 - Frequently Asked Questions*.

Types of French-fold Binding

French-fold binding is made when you fold a strip in half lengthwise; you then stitch this folded strip to your quilt, aligning the raw edges, and finally turn the folded strip to cover the raw edges. This binding can be cut on either the crosswise grain, or the bias.

Crosswise grain runs from selvage to selvage, across the width of the fabric. Binding cut on this grain will stretch somewhat, and it makes the best use of the fabric. However, it is not as durable as a bias cut binding. If the binding develops wear along the edge, it can rip along this line of wear, requiring replacement of the binding.

Bias binding runs at a 45° angle to the crosswise grain. It can stretch out of shape if you aren't careful, but that stretch is an ideal characteristic if you need to go around a curve. It's also the most durable binding you can make. Due to the diagonal crossing of the thread, if wear develops along the edge of the quilt, it just creates a hole in the binding rather than a rip, so it's much easier to repair.

Binding is almost never cut from the lengthwise grain; it's far too stiff and unforgiving. I have only ever done it with fabric that had a worthwhile design and on projects that would get little physical use.

Binding Crazy Angles: Mastering Curves, Points, Cleavage, and More

Many people think bias-cut binding doesn't use the fabric as efficiently as crosswise grain, but that's because so many instructions only tell you how to get bias binding from a square, instead of fully utilizing the fabric available.

Despite the obvious advantages of bias binding, I typically use it only for specific situations:

1. When my quilt edge is curved or irregular (bias binding will conform to the curve and lay flat when finished).

2. When the quilt will get heavy usage (great for baby quilts and picnic blankets).

3. When the fabric looks better or more interesting cut on the bias (stripes and plaids are especially fun).

For the purposes of this book, we're going to focus on bias binding. If your quilt only has straight edges (with points and cleavage), it's fine to use crosswise binding.

Calculate the Binding Strip Width

You can cut your binding at any width you want, but take into consideration the finished width of the binding you want to achieve. A proper binding is balanced on the front side and the back, with the edge of the quilt sandwich touching the inside of the binding all the way around. That's known as a "full" binding.

Unfortunately, I see a lot of quilters who just cut their binding at 2½", and stitch it with a ¼" seam allowance, regardless of what the quilt needs.

In reality, a 2½" cut binding generally yields a ⅜" finished binding, and stitching it with the wrong seam allowance can cause issues later when you're trying to make a neat finish. If you want a ⅜" finished binding - great, but if you wanted a ¼" finish instead, that 2½" cut binding won't always work to create a full binding.

A basic formula to use to calculate the cut width of your strips is:

(6 × FINISHED BINDING WIDTH) + (¼" to ½" EASE)

In French-fold binding, everything is doubled, so to get to (6) binding widths, you need to account for (2) seam allowances, (2) layers of binding on the front, and (2) layers on the back.

The extra ¼" to ½" of ease allows for the thickness of your batting and the little bit of fabric you lose in folding the binding over the edge of the quilt.

Part 2: Binding Basics

No matter what width you choose, it's important to trim your quilts correctly and set your machine to the correct seam allowance to make the binding look great.

Let's do a real example. Let's say I want a binding that finishes at ¼". How wide should I cut my strips?

(6 × ¼") + (¼" to ½" EASE) = 1½" + EASE = 1¾"- to 2"-WIDE CUT STRIPS

Wow! That's much narrower than the 2½" strips everyone cuts by default!

Also, if you have a very high-loft batting, you may need to adjust that ease measurement even more. This is why people find quilt binding so challenging: there are many variables to consider before you find the right combination that yields a full binding that looks amazing.

> *Once you learn the technique, I recommend making samples of your most commonly-used batting and fabric combinations, with the width of binding strip you want to use. You'll start to see where you need to make adjustments to get a full, balanced binding.*

Throughout the rest of the book, we will work with 2½" cut strips, since that is the most common.

Calculate the Binding Length

When you have a quilt with only straight edges, it's easy to calculate the length of the binding with the following formula:

2 × (QUILT LENGTH + QUILT WIDTH) + 15" BUFFER

However, when the quilt has irregular edges, it's a bit more challenging. I solve this by directly measuring the edges of the quilt with a flexible tape measure, and then adding about 1" for every point where the quilt changes direction and a 5" buffer. If I had to write this as a formula, it would look like this:

*(CURVED EDGE LENGTH × # OF CURVED EDGES) +
(CURVED CORNER LENGTH × # OF CORNERS) +
(LENGTH OF STRAIGHT EDGES × # OF STRAIGHT EDGES) +
1 × (# OF CURVED EDGES + # OF CORNERS + # OF STRAIGHT EDGES) +
5" BUFFER*

Binding Crazy Angles: Mastering Curves, Points, Cleavage, and More

On curves, stand the tape measure up along the edge and measure from the starting point of the curve to the end where it changes direction. (In this photo, we started in the middle of the curve just to demonstrate the tape measure position.)

If you have the same size curve around the quilt, count the number of curves. If you have curved corners, don't forget to measure them separately and add those into your numbers.

On straight edges, lay the tape measure down and measure from the starting point of the straight edge to the end where it changes direction.

If you have straight edges of the same length around the quilt, count the number of edges.

If you have multiple types of curves or lengths of straight edges, you'll need to account for these in your measurements. With so many different elements to consider, it may be faster to just measure the perimeter of the quilt instead of counting shapes!

Determine the Fabric Required

Now we just have to calculate how much fabric this will require. We need two numbers: the cut width of the binding strips and the amount of usable fabric per cut. This same formula works for both crosswise and bias binding. Let's assume that you measured a quilt and determined that it needed 235" of binding length.

For all fabrics, I assume that 40" is the usable amount of fabric (once the selvages are removed) when I cut across the width of the fabric.

Part 2: Binding Basics

Knowing this, I can divide the length of binding I need by the usable fabric amount to find out the number of strips that need to be cut. So:

235" ÷ 40" = 5.88 strips or 6 strips

Always round up to the next largest whole number, as we aren't going to work with partial strips.

To understand how much fabric is needed, you need to multiply the number of strips by the cut width of the strips, which gives you the width of the fabric in inches. This is rounded up to the nearest ⅛ yard. In our example:

6 strips × 2½" = 15", rounded up to ½ yard (18")

You should have no problem getting the amount of binding you need from the same amount of fabric, regardless of whether you are cutting crosswise or bias binding.

Below is a chart showing how much binding you can get from common cuts of fabric using 2½" cut strips. You can see that bias cutting is actually more efficient!

2½" Cut Strips

Yardage	Crosswise Binding Length Yield	Bias Binding Length Yield	Approximate Quilt Dimensions
Fat Quarter	110"	123"	27" × 27"
1/4 yard	110"	130"	27" × 27"
3/8 yard	180"	187"	45" × 45"
1/2 yard	250"	260"	62" × 62"
5/8 yard	320"	340"	80" × 80"
3/4 yard	355"	375"	88" × 88"
7/8 yard	425"	452"	106" × 106"
1 yard	495"	514"	123" × 123"

Calculations assume 40" of usable fabric after removing selvages (20" for a fat quarter)

Prepare the Binding Fabric

Whenever I cut strips, I make it a point to always straighten my fabric along the grain first. Fabric rarely comes perfectly aligned right off the bolt, so it takes a little bit of effort to make sure it is on-grain.

To straighten your fabric, first press out all wrinkles and especially the bolt-fold. You don't want this fold to make it difficult to see the true grain.

Binding Crazy Angles: Mastering Curves, Points, Cleavage, and More

Hold up the fabric by the selvages, between your fingers, keeping the selvages straight along the top.

In this photo is an exaggerated way of showing that the fabric is not on-grain, even though the selvages are straight.

It's far too common to ask for yardage off the bolt and end up being shorted due to twisted grain!

To see how far off your fabric is from being cut on-grain, hold the selvages together and align the cut edges on the left.

Notice here that with the cut edge aligned on the left, the fabric looks a little off-kilter and the folded edge is still twisted.

If we did not take the time to straighten the fabric first, our binding strips would also be twisted this way - giving the dreaded "V" or "W" shape.

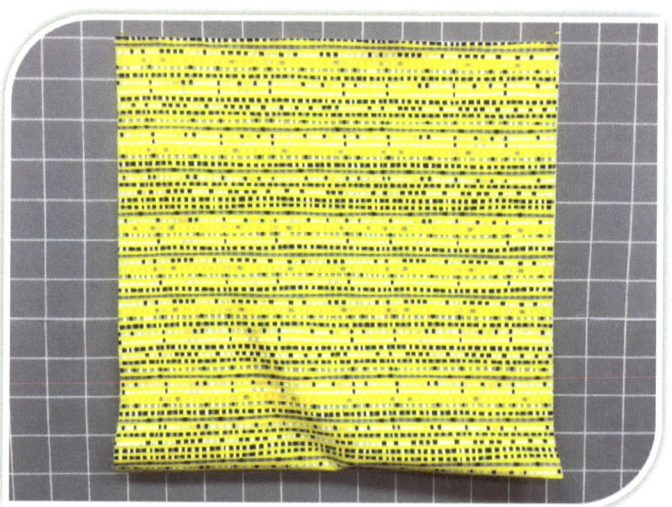

Keeping the selvages aligned, adjust the fabric until you see the twist go away and the fabric falls straight and even.

Your cut edges are no longer even, and that's okay. You've just straightened your fabric; now we have to square it!

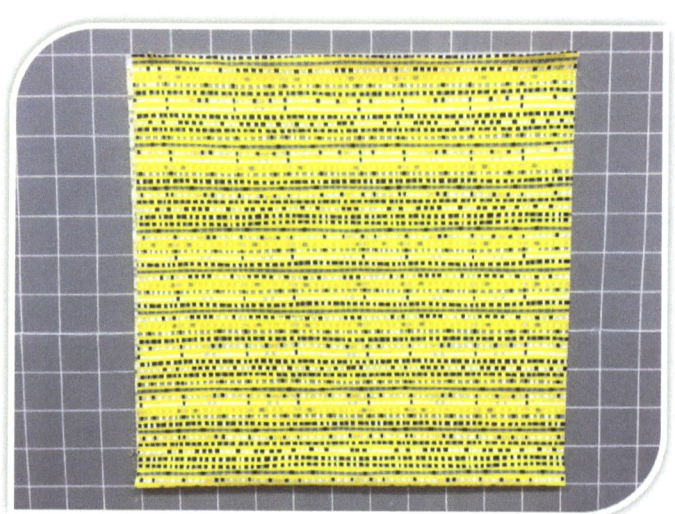

Part 2: Binding Basics

Lay your fabric on your cutting mat, preserving the straight-grain with the fold away from you.

Align your acrylic ruler with the fold and cut off one edge of the fabric (the side of your dominant hand) to make a new straight edge.

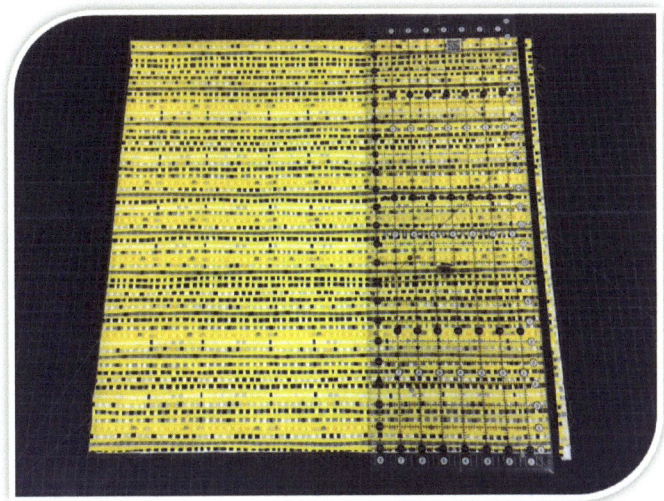

Now that you have a straight edge, rotate your fabric so that your straight edge is along the bottom and the selvages are on the side of your dominant hand.

Align your ruler with the straight edge and the fold and remove your selvages.

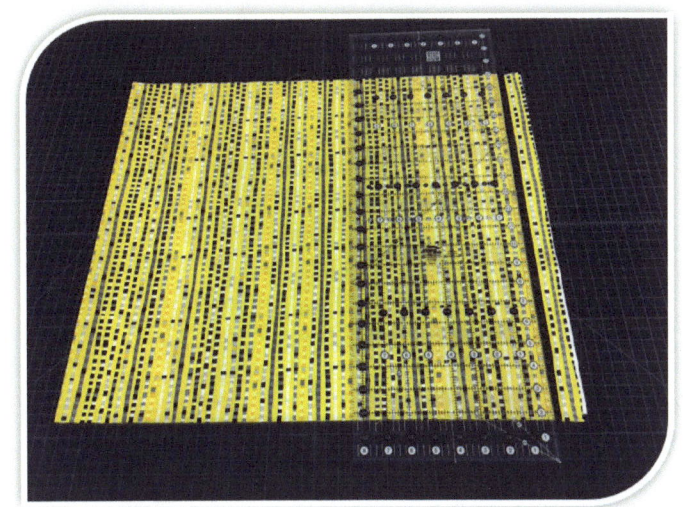

Rotate the fabric until the remaining cut edge is on the side of your dominant hand.

Align your acrylic ruler with the fold and cut off the edge of the fabric to make a new straight edge.

You now have three straight cut edges and a fold. You're ready to cut your bias binding!

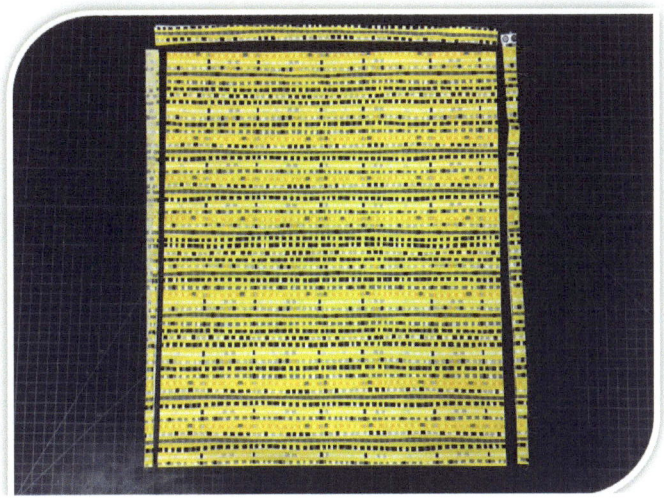

Part 3: Make Bias Binding

Bias binding is a little trickier to cut because you need to cut at a 45° angle to get the true bias grain. There are several methods for doing this, and you can choose your method depending on how much time you want to spend on the effort!

One of the most popular methods of cutting bias binding involves drawing lines, stitching fabric into a twisted tube, and then cutting it all out along the drawn lines with a pair of scissors. While this certainly is a clever way to achieve continuous binding by stitching a single seam, you're not actually cutting on the true bias.

I will focus on the simplest method that's least wasteful of fabric and time. You'll have more seams to stitch, but you can use your rotary cutter the entire time!

Cut Bias Binding Strips

In **Part 2: Binding Basics**, we straightened and squared the fabric needed for bias binding, and now it's ready to cut.

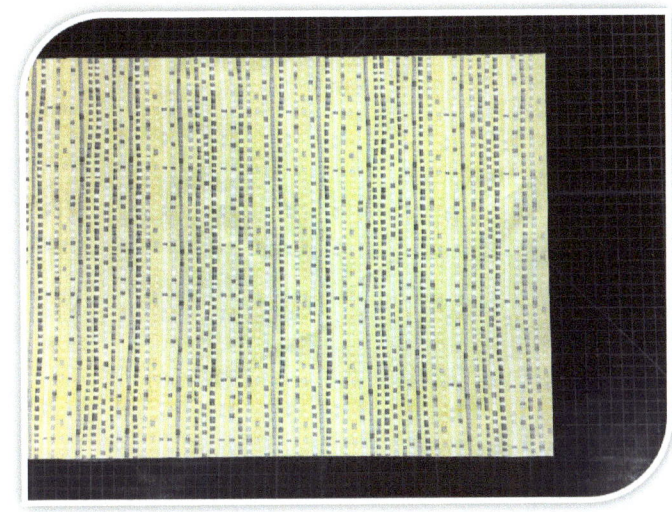

Unfold your fabric onto a cutting mat with the wrong side up, and the former selvages to your left and right.

Binding Crazy Angles: Mastering Curves, Points, Cleavage, and More

Fold the lower right corner up at an angle to meet the top raw edge. Lightly finger-press the fold.

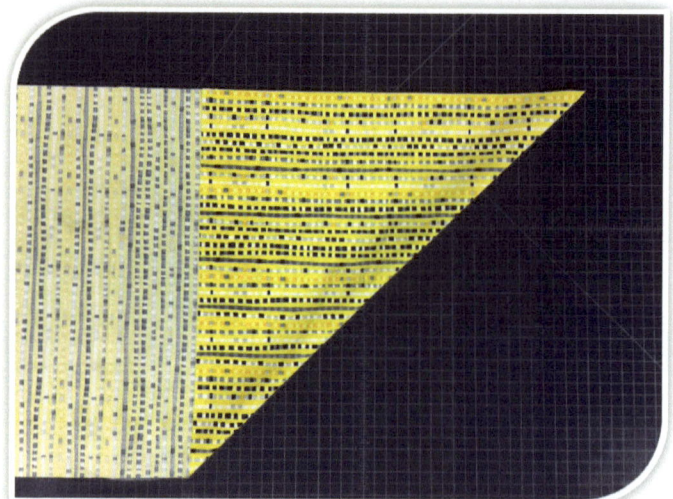

Fold the upper right corner down over the previous fold, matching points and the fold.

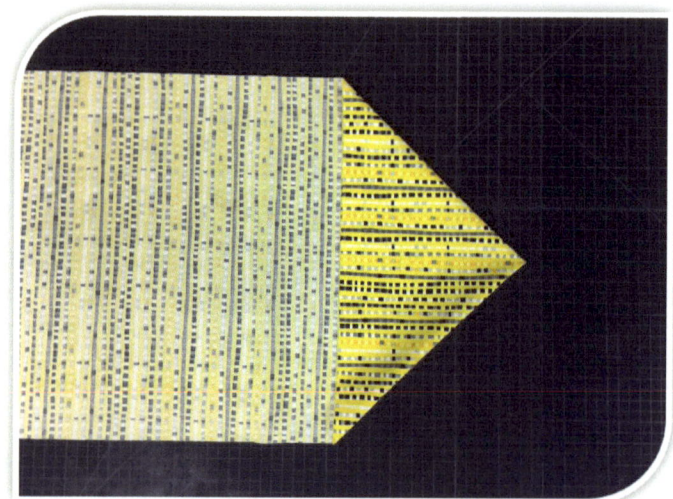

If you're working with a wider cut of yardage, you may need to fold the fabric again so it's able to be cut with your ruler.

To do this, fold down the upper right edge, keeping all the folds aligned.

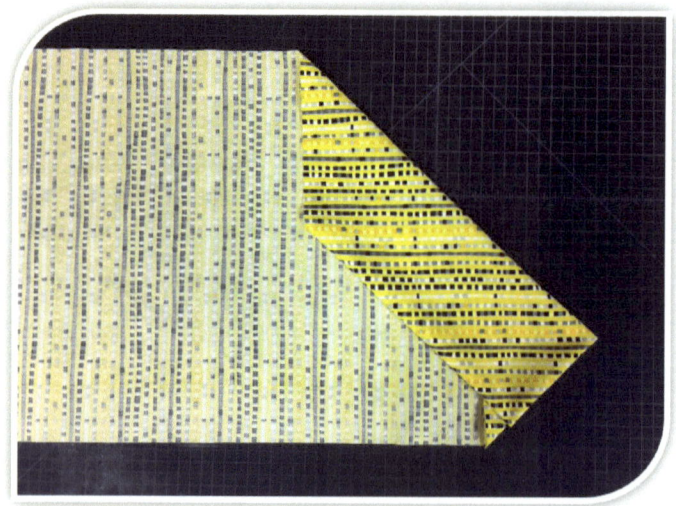

Part 3: Make Bias Binding

Rotate the fabric with the folds toward your dominant hand, keeping folds aligned.

Align your ruler close to the folded edge of the fabric, and cut off the tiniest sliver of fabric through all layers.

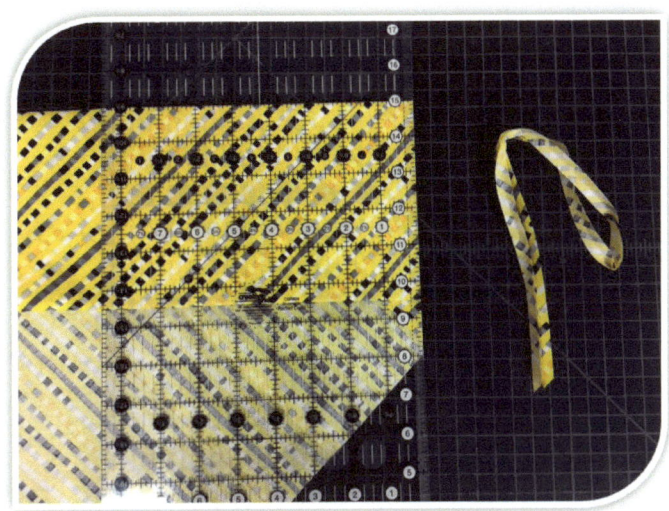

Rotate the fabric 180° so the bulk of the fabric is up toward your right.

Align your ruler on the mark that represents your chosen strip width (2½" in our example). Cut through all layers.

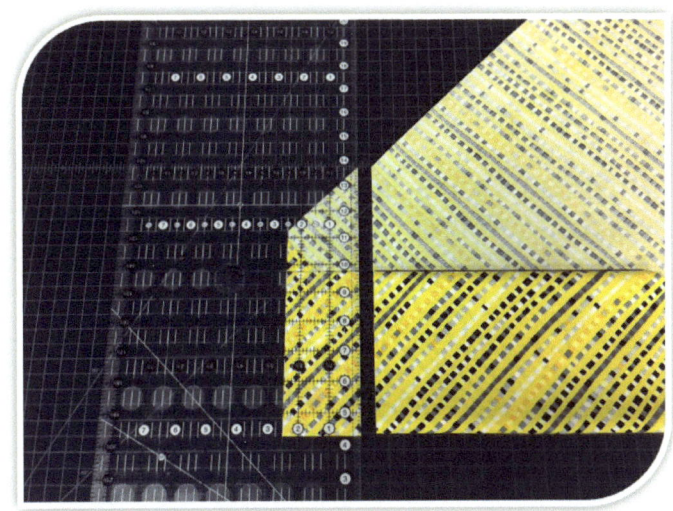

Continue cutting strips until the fabric is too small to reasonably work as binding, or until you reach a point where the fabric is longer than your ruler.

Binding Crazy Angles: Mastering Curves, Points, Cleavage, and More

If needed, to continue cutting, fold the remaining fabric wrong sides together, keeping the cut edge aligned, until it fits into your ruler's cutting field.

Continue cutting strips in this manner until the fabric is too small to reasonably work as binding.

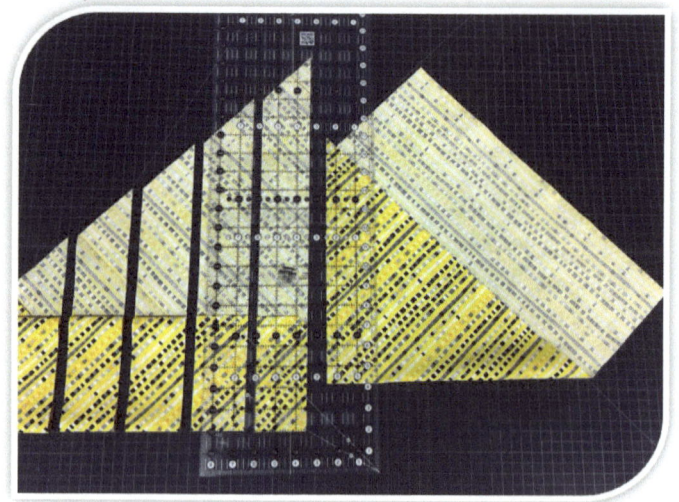

Stack several binding strips, carefully aligning the angled edges.

Using the LoveBug Studios Binding Tool, face up so the text is readable, align the tool with the angled side of each stack.

Cut off the exposed fabric to the right of the tool through all layers, to dog-ear the corners.

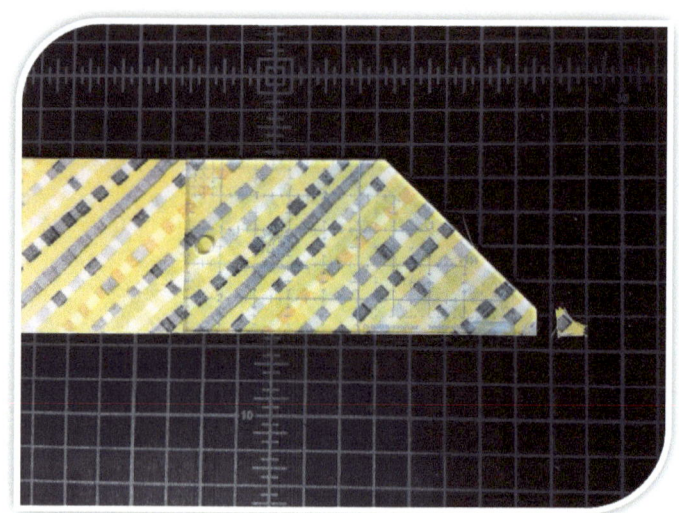

Sew Bias Binding Strips

Once all of your strips are cut, you'll have two types of cut strips. Before you start sewing, you need to understand how to handle these so that you can get one continuous strip without having to re-cut any of the binding ends.

Type 1 strips will have the angled ends facing the same direction.

Part 3: Make Bias Binding

Sort these strips together. These will essentially be sewn end to end, so that their angles will match.

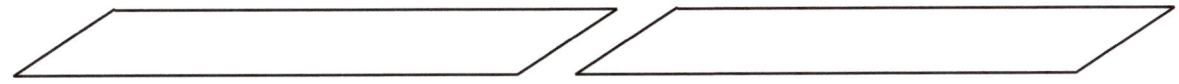

Type 2 strips will have the angled ends facing opposite directions.

To stitch these, rotate every other strip, then sew them end to end, in order to get the angles to match.

When you're stitching the strips, stitch each type together independently. For your final seam, you'll need to match one end of the Type 1 strip length with the corresponding end of the Type 2 strip length.

In the event that you need to re-cut one of the angled ends, you can use the Binding Tool to square off the end and re-cut it to the proper angle.

To stitch the strips together (either Type 1 or Type 2), lay them right sides together, so that they meet at a 90° angle, and the dog-eared corners match.

Set up your machine to stitch a ¼" seam allowance.

Stitch all the diagonal seams in the binding,

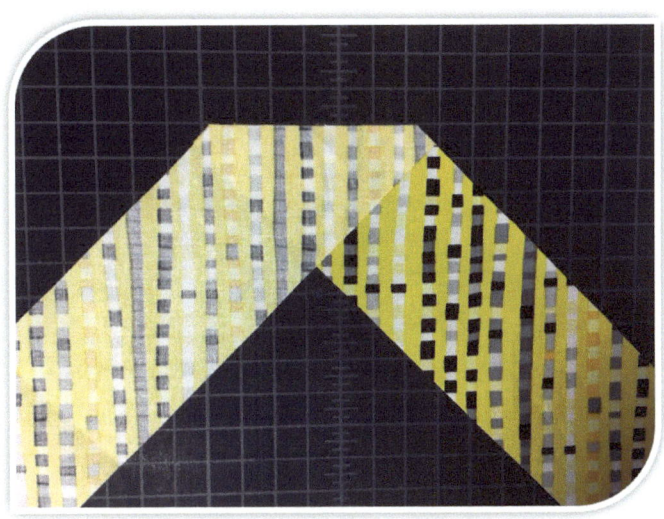

Binding Crazy Angles: Mastering Curves, Points, Cleavage, and More

Set up your machine to stitch a ¼" seam allowance.

Stitch all the diagonal seams in the binding.

Press Binding Strips

For this step, you'll want a good pressing surface and a hot, dry iron.

Try to avoid using steam, water, or starch at this stage so you don't distort your binding fabric - especially if it's cut on the bias.

Press all the seams open to reduce bulk.

You can press all the seams open at once, or press them as you go. For my own process, I press as I go; it means handling the strips less, and that reduces the opportunities for distortion.

Part 3: Make Bias Binding

Fold the binding strip in half widthwise, right side out, and press along the length, being careful not to stretch or distort it.

As you work, carefully wind the pressed binding around an empty cardboard tube or spool to protect it from stretching.

A fun way to store your finished binding is on Binding Babies®!

Part 4: Prepare to Bind the Quilt

Now that we've prepared our binding, we're almost ready to attach the binding to the quilt. This is where your results are going to vary, and the first time you do this, you'll want to conduct a couple of experiments to get the settings correct for your project. Your binding attachment will vary based on a few factors:

- type of fabric (cotton, flannel, or plush);
- type of batting (high, medium, or low loft); and
- type of quilt (pieced to the edge, with or without borders, etc.).

If you change any of these variables, you'll need to repeat these steps to make sure you get the best results on each project.

Prep, Baste and Trim the Quilt

When you make a quilt, the batting and backing extend beyond the quilt top, and this will eventually need to be trimmed off. Before we do that, we need to prep, baste, and trim the quilt based on the type of quilt and look you want to achieve.

To prep the quilt, evaluate whether or not it needs to be blocked. Sometimes quilting can introduce wonkiness and waviness into the quilt so that it's no longer flat and square. If your quilt waves at you where you don't want it to, your binding will too! The process to return the quilt to flat and square is called, "blocking". You'll want to do this even on quilts that you haven't cut crazy angles into yet.

Not all quilts require blocking; I typically only do this for quilts that will be hung to exhibit or need to be photographed. The quilt has to be dampened, measured and manipulated to make it flat and square, and then left to dry. You need a flat, clean, pinnable surface, and the time and space to do the blocking from start to finish.

If you need to learn how to block your quilt, check out the Resources chapter at the end of the book for further instruction.

Binding Crazy Angles: Mastering Curves, Points, Cleavage, and More

If you're planning to cut crazy angles and curves into your quilt, many books and patterns will tell you not to cut into the quilt until after you apply the binding. I find that bindings are neater and more successful if they've been trimmed first.

Before we do the trimming, we need to baste the quilt along the desired binding path to secure all the edges.

For quilts where the binding path is built into the pattern - like hexagons, pointed table runners, or circular tree skirts, following this path is easy. For quilts where you want to create a path - like scallops - you have to plan for them in advance. This book assumes you already know how to do that; if you don't and you're interested in learning, check out the Resources chapter at the end of the book.

To add basting, use your zipper foot and the longest stitch length your machine allows (mine is 6.0mm).

Stitch around the edge of your quilt ⅛" from the edge of the quilt top, all around the perimeter (black stitched line). Alternatively, if you're creating the binding path, draw your desired path on the quilt, and then baste along this line. Do this **before** trimming your quilt.

In the example used in the book, we used pre-quilted fabric, so there wasn't "extra" batting and backing to trim. The rule still applies though; before you cut off any part of your quilt, you need to baste the raw edges, or baste the shape you're planning to cut, in order to secure the three layers of your quilt.

Once this is complete, you can cut away the excess batting and backing from the quilt right next to your line of basting.

One caveat to this: if your quilt has piecing all the way out to the edge and you need to preserve the correct seam allowance so you don't cut off points in your design, you might need to plan differently for how you cut the quilt or your binding.

Part 4: Prepare to Bind the Quilt

If your piecing goes out to the edge and you want to preserve your points and intersections, you can either:

Trim the quilt next to the edge, and cut your binding width to a size that is compatible with a ¼" seam allowance; or

Trim your quilt ⅛" from the edge of the quilt top, and cut your binding width to a size that is compatible with a ⅜" seam allowance.

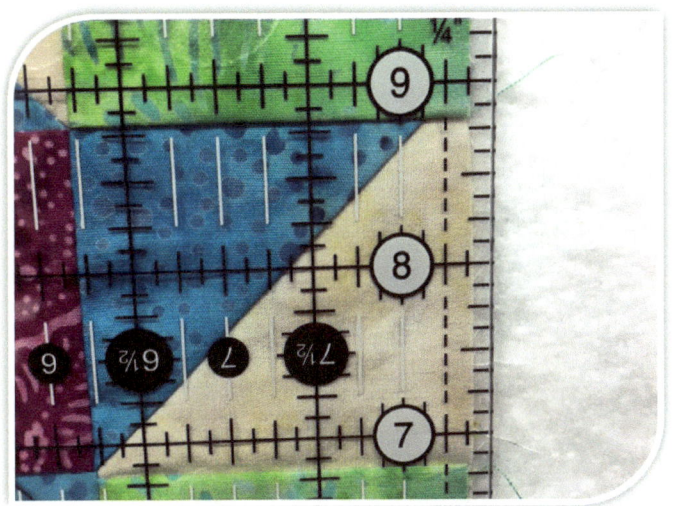

Test Machine Settings

Before we permanently attach the binding to the quilt, let's play with our machine settings so we stitch on the binding accurately. We want to make sure all the settings are correct, so that when we turn the binding to the back, it's balanced on the front and back and covers your stitching without crushing the edge or leaving empty space.

Start with the Edge Stitching Foot. Set your machine to a long basting stitch using a contrasting thread, 75/11 needle, and with the needle to the far right (6.0mm is the stitch length; 3.5 is the right needle position on my machine).

If your machine doesn't allow you to move the needle, use a bit of masking tape to mark a sewing guide on the bed of your machine.

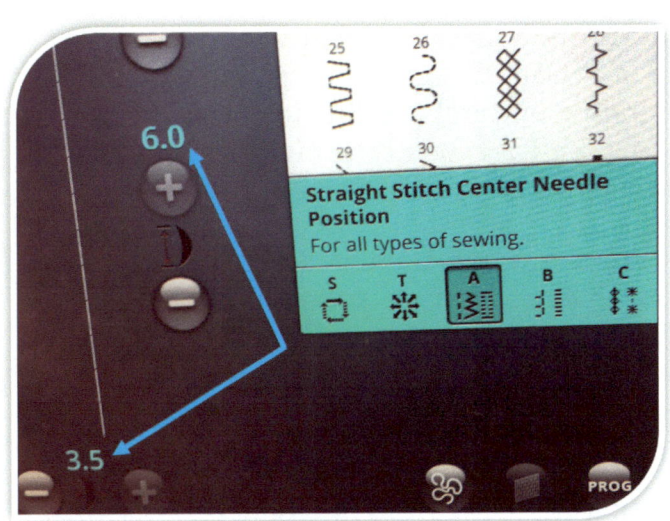

Do you use different battings or binding widths on your projects? It may be a good idea to make up some small samples so you can play with this technique. Use a permanent fabric pen to write down your settings on each sample; next time you use that combination, you'll already know what to do!

Binding Crazy Angles: Mastering Curves, Points, Cleavage, and More

The exact measurement from the needle to the edge of the foot isn't as critical as being able to identify and replicate it once you get the right settings.

First, align the raw edge of the **front** of your quilt sandwich with the raw edges of your binding. Stitch 2-3" with the basting stitch and remove it from the machine.

The "where" doesn't matter; you'll likely be removing these stitches!

> *If you trimmed your quilt with the batting and backing flush with the edge of the quilt top, align the binding with this edge. If you trimmed the batting and backing a distance away from the quilt top, align the binding with the edge of the batting and backing.*

Fold this test section to the back of the quilt and test the fit. You want the quilt sandwich to fill the binding without needing to yank on it. You also want the binding to slightly cover the stitches.

In this example, there is clearly too much extra binding turned to the back, so I need to move my needle (or my guide).

What we're trying to find here is the seam allowance that will give us the best balance of fabric on the front and the back, cover our stitching line, and look just as good on both sides of the quilt. **It should be close to, but may not be exactly, the finished binding width we calculated in Part 2.**

Part 4: Prepare to Bind the Quilt

Whenever you're testing your binding attachment settings, too much fabric on the back indicates moving your needle left to take up more of the binding strip. Not enough fabric on the back indicates moving your needle right to take up less fabric.

Remove the basting stitches, and try again with a different needle position.

Since there is too much fabric turned to the back, I need to move my needle left.

In this example, the machine is still set to the 6.0mm basting stitch, but the needle has been moved left (all the way to the 0.0 center position.)

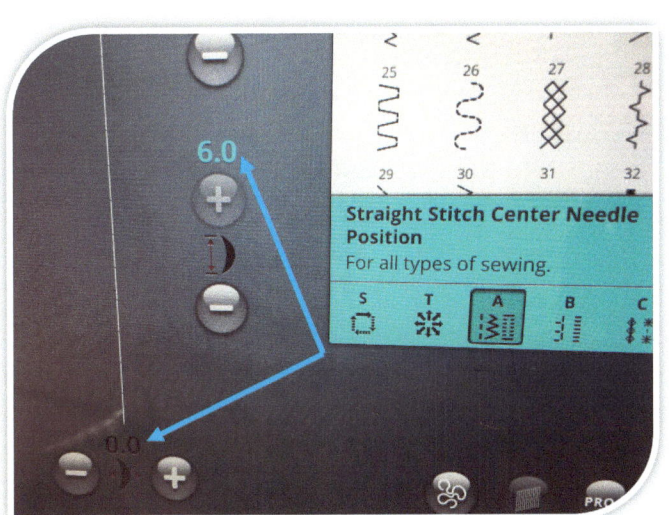

If you are testing your machine settings moving only right to left, you can leave your basting stitches in, because they won't interfere with your next test. The moment you move left to right, you must pull out the basting as it will prevent you from testing the next adjustment.

Again, align the raw edge of the front of your quilt sandwich with the raw edges of your binding. Stitch another 2-3" with the new setting.

Binding Crazy Angles: Mastering Curves, Points, Cleavage, and More

Fold this test section to the back of the quilt and test the fit.

In this example, there's enough binding to cover the stitches, so we don't need to make any other adjustments.

If the binding didn't cover the stitches here, we would need to move the needle (or the guide) to the right, to take up less fabric.

Use the gridded corner of the Binding Tool to measure the seam allowance from the basting stitch to the edge of the quilt.

Make note of this seam allowance - you'll be using it often!

If your seam allowance is between markings, use a piece of masking tape on the ruler to mark the measurement.

Remove the basting stitches holding the binding to the quilt. Open up the binding and fold down a ¼" hem to the inside. Press this hem in place.

If your binding tail is angled the opposite way, it's fine! You don't have to redo it.

Part 4: Prepare to Bind the Quilt

Fold the binding in half again and press the binding flat.

To start your binding, choose a section on your quilt that has at least 8" of straight edge, and start your stitching about 4" from the loose end of your binding tail.

Align the raw edges of the binding with the edge of your project.

If the only place for you to start is on a curve, try to find the straightest section you can and start away from any cleavage (inside points).

Every machine is different, as is every quilt. Don't assume your settings will be the same as mine. The point here is for you to understand, with your own sewing machine and your quilt in front of you, how to make adjustments to get your chosen binding to work. It may take more than 2 tries!

If instead of a 2½" binding strip, you decide to cut a 2" strip instead, you may find that the far right needle position is nearly perfect. The point is that only you will know for sure, and only by trying.

Write Down Your Needle Position:_____

Write Down Your Seam Allowance:_____

Part 5: Binding Wide Angles

It's the moment you've been waiting for! We've spent all this time building up to this point: attaching the binding to the quilt and tackling some of these crazy angles.

For this step, and in the subsequent chapters, you'll need your prepared binding, a couple of pins, binding clips, the Binding Tool, chalk, hand sewing needles and thread that matches your binding. The closer in shade you get, the less your stitches will show.

Wind a bobbin, thread your machine, and let's do this.

What is a Wide Angle?

For the purposes of this book, a wide angle is any outside point on a quilt where two straight sides come together at an angle of 90° or more. They are also known as "right and obtuse angles" - anything between 90° and 180°. These angles include your regular square and rectangular corners, and also corners on shapes like hexagons, octagons, the wide sides of diamonds, etc.

I'm only going to show one wide angle here, but the same principles and steps apply to any wide angle - including square corners.

Getting Started with Wide Angles

With your perfect setting achieved, reduce the stitch length from the basting stitch to one more appropriate – I use 2.0mm as the length. Your needle position should be set to what you wrote down in the previous chapter. Set your machine to stop with the needle down, and if you have the option, hover the presser foot so that it lifts when you stop.

Binding Crazy Angles: Mastering Curves, Points, Cleavage, and More

Mark the Wide Angle and Stitch the Binding

Before we start stitching, it's important to identify and mark the corner seam allowance so that we stop stitching in the correct place.

Recalling the seam allowance measurement you wrote down from the previous chapter, use the Binding Tool and chalk to mark the seam allowance on one edge near the corner.

If you're using a chalk liner, angle the liner away from the ruler so the wheel butts up against the ruler.

Repeat this step on the adjacent side, making sure the chalk lines intersect near the corner.

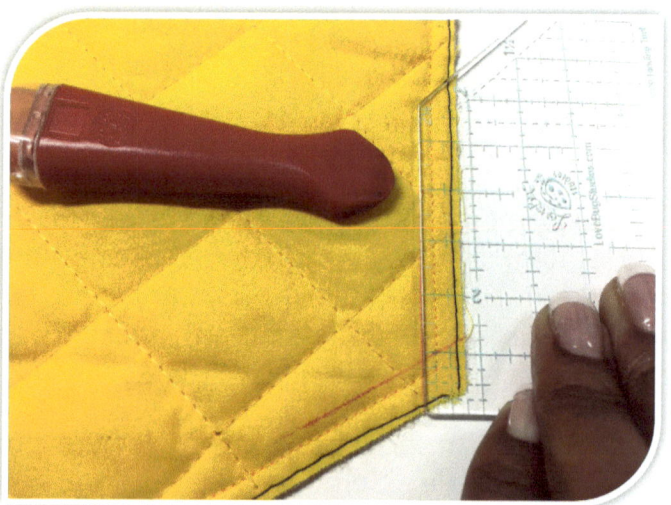

Part 5: Binding Angles

Insert a pin into the point of the intersection, making sure that the pin is perpendicular to the direction of your sewing.

The Binding Tool placed on the right edge of the project can help you make sure the pin is inserted perfectly straight.

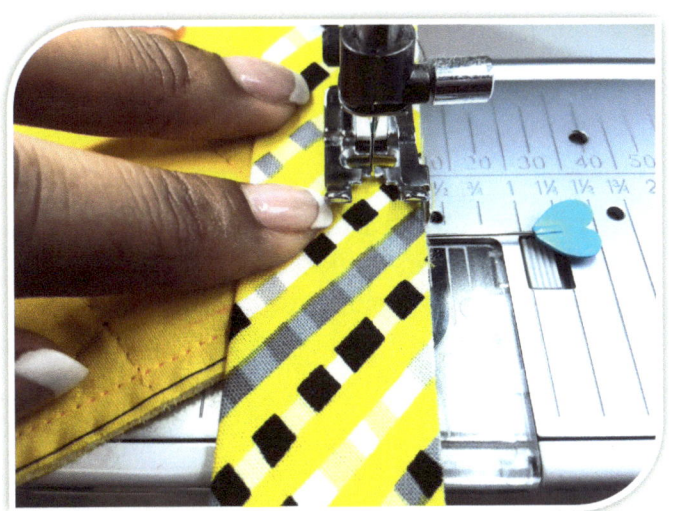

As you stitch on the binding and approach a corner, pay attention to the position of your stitching relative to the corner. Slow down as you approach the pin marking your pivot point.

Stop with your needle down when the pin is in line with your needle.

On many modern sewing machines, your throat plate has a horizontal line which is in line with the needle. If you're having a hard time seeing where the needle is relative to the pin, just sew until the pin is over this horizontal line.

If you don't have this line on your stitch plate, you can mark it with a piece of masking tape.

Binding Crazy Angles: Mastering Curves, Points, Cleavage, and More

Pivot the quilt clockwise so the corner is facing you and is directly in line with the needle. Stitch toward the corner to the end, stop, and clip your threads.

This very simple step is going to help you get your corner correct, with the right amount of fabric prepared for turning.

Note how you have a straight stitch, and then an angled stitch at the bottom off to the corner.

Use that angle as a guide to fold the binding back over your stitching line at the corner, so that the raw edge of your binding forms a straight line with the raw edge of your quilt.

Use the long edge of the Binding Tool to make sure you're folding the binding in a straight line.

-42-

Part 5: Binding Angles

Fold the binding down so it covers the next side of the quilt and the fold is even and square with the corner point of the quilt (blue arrow). Pin the corner in place.

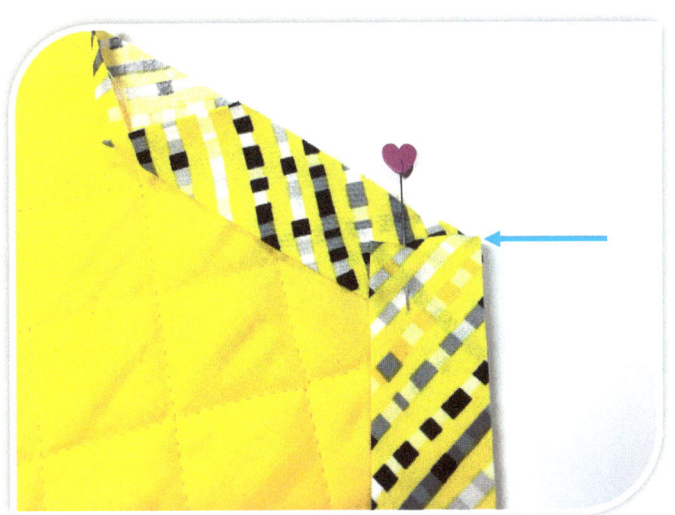

Take the time to make sure your fold here is even and square relative to the corner. If your fold is too high, as shown here (blue arrow marks the corner) there will be too much fabric in the corner and it will look overly pointed.

If your fold is too low, there won't be enough fabric and the corner will round off.

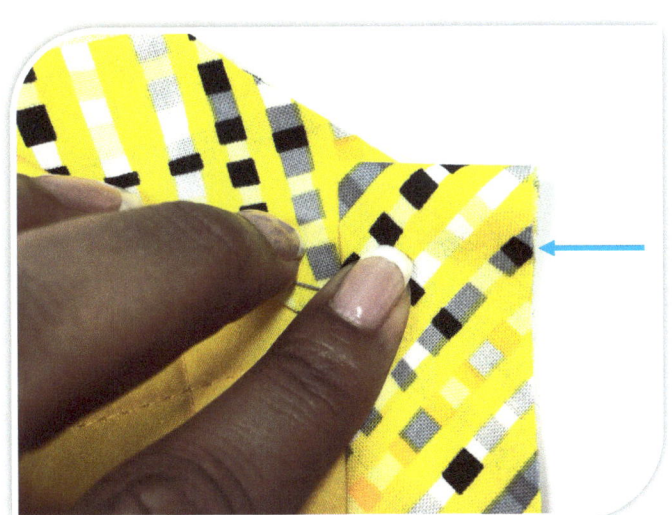

Starting from the edge of the quilt, continue stitching the binding to the quilt in this manner.

If your next corner is an angle, repeat the steps for marking and folding each corner the same way.

If your next corner is different, see one of the later chapters for marking and turning that type of corner.

Binding Crazy Angles: Mastering Curves, Points, Cleavage, and More

Finish the Wide Angle Binding

Turning the corners on wide angle binding is easy once you've done the hard work of getting the correct amount of fabric into the corner.

It's a good idea to check the fold of your corner to make sure it is going to turn correctly before you stitch too much further on your project.

Ideally, your fold will be balanced and the folds will meet in the center of the corner, essentially bisecting the angle there. If the corner was a 90° square corner, we would refer to this bisection as a mitered corner. Isn't math fun?

Push the binding away from the quilt and you will see the folded corner form on the front side of the binding.

As you continue pushing the binding away from the front and over the top, you can observe how your folds are laying.

As you look at this fold, it should be overlapping evenly with the bulk contained inside the corner.

Part 5: Binding Angles

Using one of the binding clips, fold the right side to the back and clip the binding near the corner.

Use your fingers to press the fabric down in the corner, and fold down the left side to cover the stitches.

Use another binding clip to hold the left side in place, and pin the corner flap to the quilt to hold it in place until you can stitch it closed.

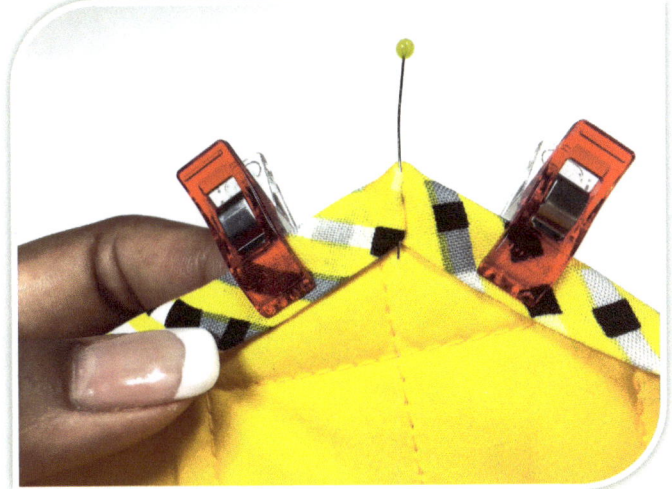

Thread your hand sewing needle with matching thread, and use a blind stitch to secure the binding to the back of the quilt, removing clips as you go.

Binding Crazy Angles: Mastering Curves, Points, Cleavage, and More

When you get to the corner, insert your needle into the bottom of the corner flap and take one or two stitches to secure it in place.

It's a good idea to stitch the flap down on the back and the front to keep it folded properly.

After stitching the miter, continue stitching along the binding until you come to the next corner.

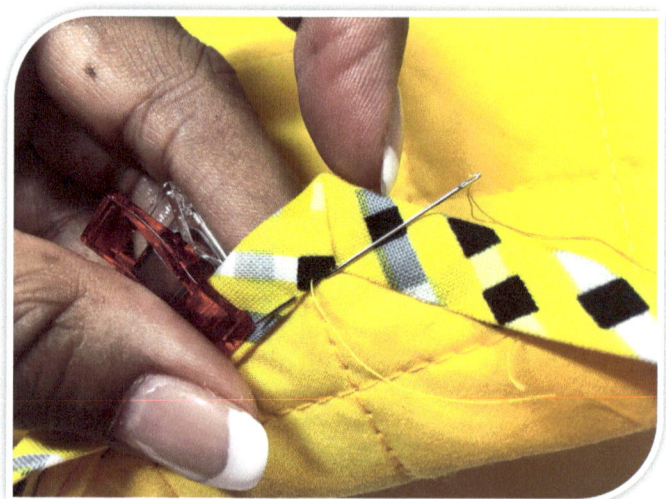

If your next corner is a wide angle, repeat the steps for marking and folding each corner the same way.

If your next corner is different, see one of the later chapters for finishing that type of corner.

Part 5: Binding Angles

Your binding should be well-balanced on the front and the back, with neat, flat corners.

Behind the Scenes:
One of the cardinal laws of quilting states that for every four corners of binding you attach, one of them will have the seam of the joined binding strips in it. It turned out to be true on this project while writing the book!

Part 6: Binding Points

What is a Point?

In this book, a point is any outside point on a quilt where two straight sides come together at an angle less than 90°. They are also known as "acute angles". These points include triangles, those found on stars, the narrow sides of diamonds and kites, etc.

If it's pointed, you can use this technique to bind it.

Getting Started with Points

You need the same supplies and machine settings as covered in the previous chapter.

Mark the Point and Stitch the Binding

As with angles, we need to identify and mark the corner seam allowance on the point so that we stop stitching in the correct place.

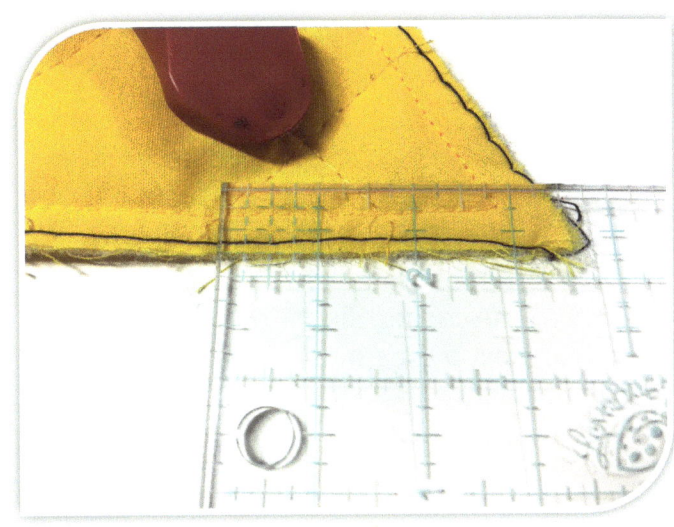

Recalling the seam allowance measurement you wrote down from the previous chapter, use the Binding Tool and chalk to mark the seam allowance on one edge near the corner.

If you're using a chalk liner, angle the liner away from the ruler so the wheel butts up against the ruler.

Binding Crazy Angles: Mastering Curves, Points, Cleavage, and More

Repeat this step on the adjacent side, making sure the chalk lines intersect near the corner.

Insert a pin into the point of the intersection, making sure that the pin is perpendicular to the direction of your sewing.

The Binding Tool placed on the right edge of the project can help you make sure the pin is inserted perfectly straight.

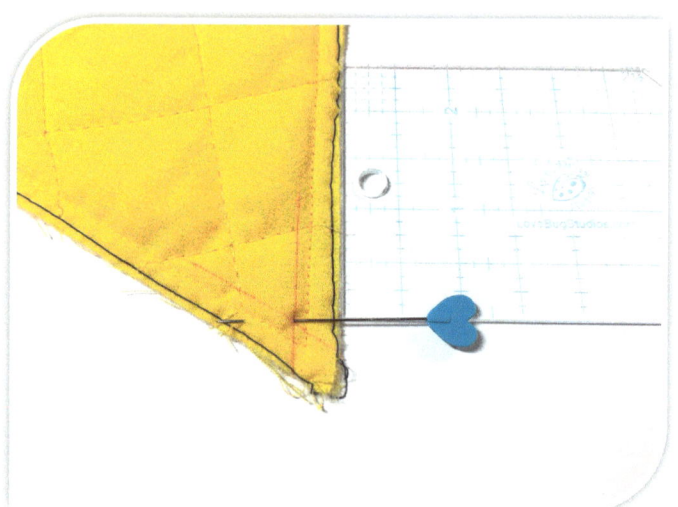

As you stitch on the binding and approach a corner, pay attention to the position of your stitching relative to the corner. Slow down as you approach the pin marking your pivot point.

Part 6: Binding Points

Stop with your needle down when the pin is in line with your needle.

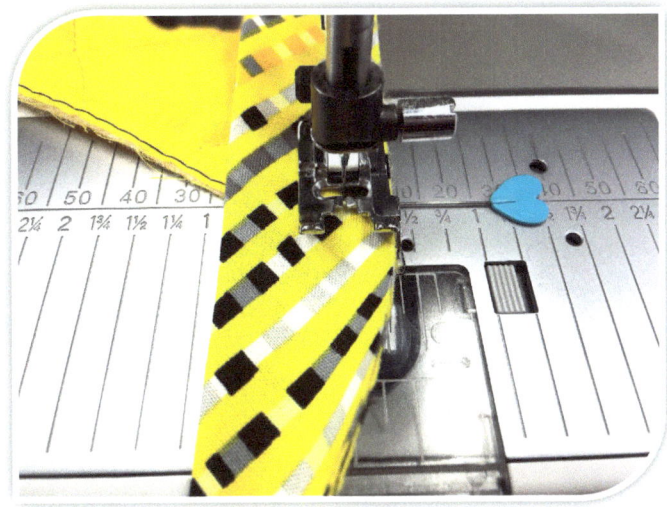

Pivot the quilt clockwise so the corner is facing you and is slightly offset from the needle.

Ideally, your stitches will fall one or two threads to the right of center. This undercuts the corner just enough to shift the bulk of the binding so that your corner is pointed.

Stitch toward the corner to the end, stop, and clip your threads.

Note how you have a straight stitch, and then an angled stitch at the bottom off to the corner.

Binding Crazy Angles: Mastering Curves, Points, Cleavage, and More

Use that angle as a guide to fold the binding back over your stitching line at the corner, so that the raw edge of your binding forms a straight line with the raw edge of your quilt.

Use the long edge of the Binding Tool to make sure you're folding the binding in a straight line.

Fold the binding down so it covers the next side of the quilt and the fold is even and square with the corner point of the quilt (blue arrow). Pin the corner in place. Your binding will extend above the edge of the quilt.

If your fold is too high, there will be too much fabric in the point and you won't be able to form the corner.

If your fold is too low, there won't be enough fabric and the point will round off.

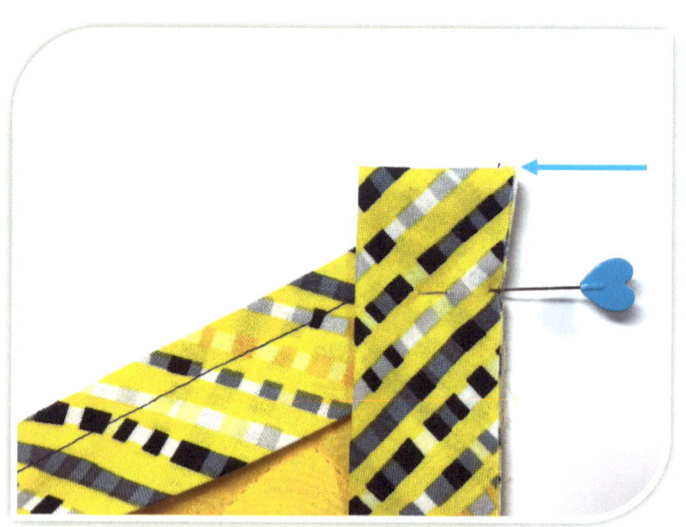

Starting from the edge of the quilt, continue stitching the binding to the quilt in this manner.

If your next corner is a point, repeat the steps for marking and folding each corner the same way.

If your next corner is different, see one of the other chapters for marking and turning that type of corner.

Part 6: Binding Points

Finish the Pointed Binding

Turning the corners on pointed binding is a little trickier than for other types of corners, but once you get the hang of it, you'll never be intimidated by any crazy angle again.

It's a good idea to check the fold of your corner to make sure it is going to turn correctly before you stitch too much further on your project.

As with angles, you want your fold to be balanced and meet in the center of the corner. The point should be sharp and straight.

Push the binding away from the quilt and you will see the folded corner form on the front side of the binding.

As you continue pushing the binding away from the front and over the top, you can observe how your folds are laying.

As you look at this fold, it should be overlapping evenly but it won't be contained inside the corner. We need to address that.

Binding Crazy Angles: Mastering Curves, Points, Cleavage, and More

If you turn the binding to the back, you'll see how the bulk of the binding on one side extends above the quilt (blue arrow). This will distort your corner.

We will remove everything above the dotted blue line.

Cut this bulk carefully, straight across, with a sharp pair of scissors.

Don't get aggressive; more is not better. If you cut too deeply, you'll create a hole on the front side of your binding, and you'll have to redo the binding here.

Using one of the binding clips, fold the right side of the binding to the back and clip the binding near the corner.

Use your fingers to press the fabric down in the corner.

Part 6: Binding Points

On the left side, you will have a little extra fabric to fold in; take the fold on the left and fold it in so it touches the raw edge of the quilt.

Don't yank on this too much so you don't expose the hole you cut in the corner.

Use a pin or another binder clip if you need help keeping the fabric flat while you fold the corner.

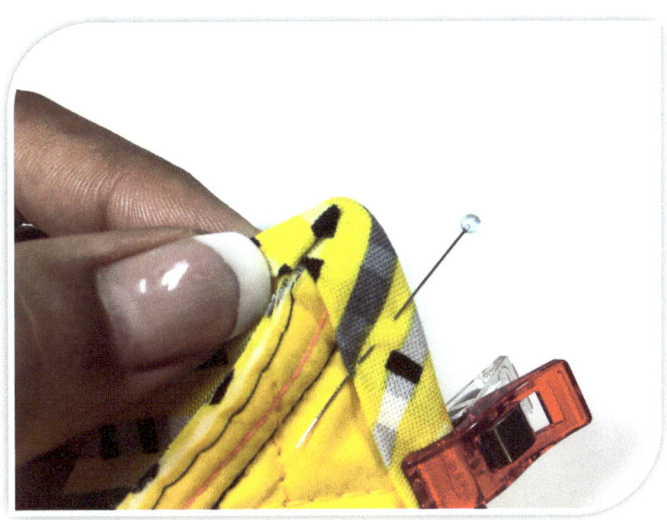

Here is an unobstructed view of what your corner will look like when you fold down the bulk of the corner.

Fold down the left side to cover the stitches.

Use another binding clip to hold the left side in place, and pin the corner flap to the quilt to hold it in place until you can stitch it closed.

Binding Crazy Angles: Mastering Curves, Points, Cleavage, and More

Thread your hand sewing needle with matching thread, and use a blind stitch to secure the binding to the back of the quilt, removing clips as you go.

When you get to the corner, insert your needle into the bottom of the corner flap and take one or two stitches to secure it in place.

It's a good idea to stitch the flap down on the back and the front to keep it folded properly and protect the hole that was created by debulking the corner in a previous step.

After stitching the miter, continue stitching along the binding until you come to the next corner.

If your next corner is a point, repeat the steps for marking and folding each corner the same way.

If your next corner is different, see one of the other chapters for finishing that type of corner.

Part 6: Binding Points

Your binding should be well-balanced on the front and the back, with a sharp, pointed corner.

Part 7: Binding Curves

Of all the crazy angles there are, you'll find curves to be a cakewalk after tackling the other techniques in this book.

The main requirement for curves is bias binding; once you have that, binding a curve is about as easy as binding a straight line.

Inside curves and outside curves are treated the same way: it's all about easing!

Getting Started with Curves

You need the same supplies and machine settings as covered in the previous chapters. You might want to have a few more binding clips on hand!

Stitch Curved Binding

The great thing about curves is that there are no corners! At least, not until you come to one.

If you are working on a quilt without straight edges, you'll need to start the binding somewhere.

Pick an area on the curve that's relatively flat, and pin a few inches of the binding to the curve. Gently ease the binding around the curve.

Remember to start about 4" from the starting tail of the binding.

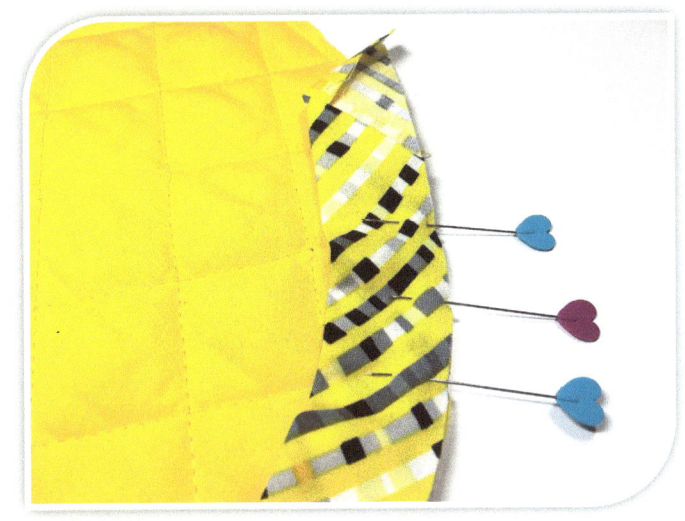

Binding Crazy Angles: Mastering Curves, Points, Cleavage, and More

Stitch the binding to the curve, as you ease the binding around it.

Don't yank on the binding or stretch it too much out of shape, but make sure you are easing the binding and not preventing it from laying flat along the edge.

If you're getting tucks and puckers, you're not easing enough around the curve.

If the binding is standing up away from the quilt, you're easing too much.

> **Binding Scallops:**
> On the edges of quilts, scallops are a combination of the curve and cleavage techniques. Depending on how you decide to scallop your corners, you may also need the point technique as well.

Finish the Curved Binding

Once you get the binding stitched to the quilt, pull the binding over the top edge and use binding clips to help you keep the binding folded toward the quilt.

You may see some extra fullness in between the binding clips; you need to ease in this fullness as you go. The clips can help you distribute this fullness.

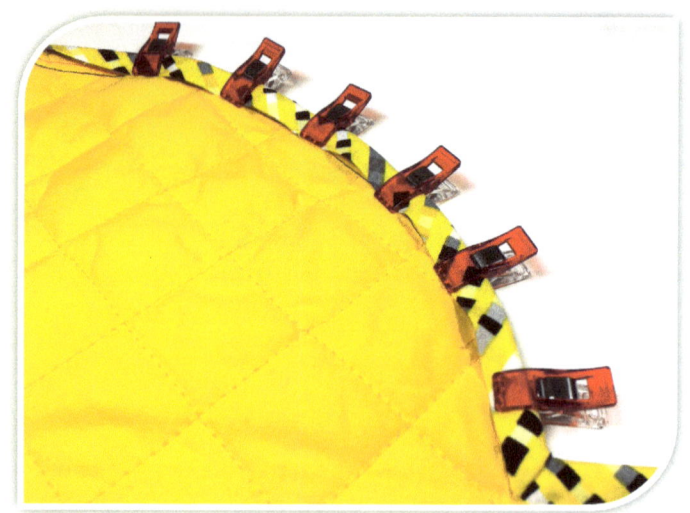

Part 7: Binding Curves

Thread your hand sewing needle with matching thread, and use a blind stitch to secure the binding to the back of the quilt, removing clips as you go.

Continue using clips to hold the binding while stitching the binding to the quilt.

If you are not binding a circle, you'll probably need one of the other chapters for finishing the next corner you come to.

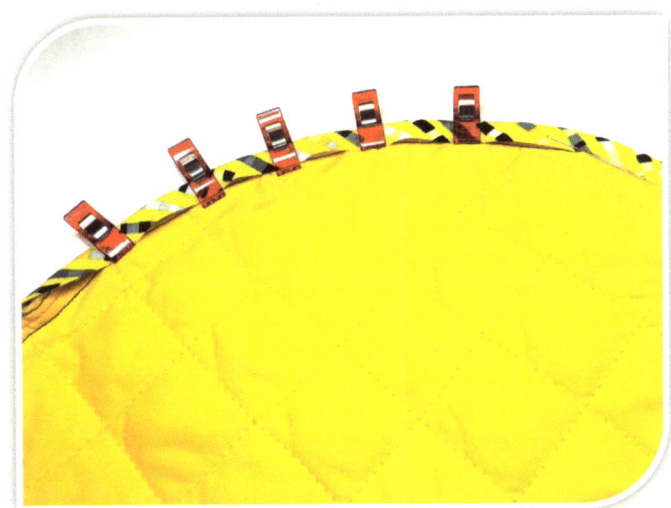

Your binding should be well-balanced on the front and the back, with the curve laying flat.

Part 8: Binding Cleavage

What is Cleavage?

Simply put, cleavage is any angle that points inward on a shape. Think of a heart shape, and the point where the two lobes meet at the top; that's cleavage.

Interestingly, no matter what angle of cleavage you're dealing with, they are all stitched the same way. The deeper the angle, the more fussy it will be to stitch the overlap, but it's completely doable.

Getting Started with Cleavage

You need the same supplies and machine settings as covered in the previous chapters.

Mark the Cleavage and Stitch the Binding

As with angles and points, we need to identify and mark the corner seam allowance on the inside point so that we stop stitching in the correct place.

Recalling the seam allowance measurement you wrote down from a previous chapter, use the Binding Tool and chalk to mark the seam allowance on one edge near the inside point.

Binding Crazy Angles: Mastering Curves, Points, Cleavage, and More

If you're using a chalk liner, angle the liner away from the ruler so the wheel butts up against the ruler.

Repeat this step on the adjacent side, making sure the chalk lines intersect near the inside point.

Using a sharp pair of scissors or snips, clip the seam allowance from the outside edge of the cleavage up to the inside point that you marked.

Be careful not to clip past this point or you will create a hole at the edge of your quilt.

If you're worried about it, you can sew reinforcement stitches just inside the line.

Begin stitching the binding to the quilt, stopping about 3" from the inside point.

Using the Binding Tool and the chalk marker, transfer the seam markings from the edges of the cleavage.

Part 8: Binding Cleavage

Pin the binding to the quilt so that the point you marked stays aligned as you stitch.

Use your stiletto, if needed, to help you ease in the binding.

Stop with your needle down when you reach the pin.

Remove the pin marking the point.

Using the cut seam, open up the quilt so that the left and right edges of the cleavage form a straight line ahead of and behind the needle.

You will need to maneuver the bulk of the quilt to the left so that you don't stitch a pleat or any puckers into this point.

Backstitch over this area to reinforce the stitching at the cut point.

Binding Crazy Angles: Mastering Curves, Points, Cleavage, and More

Finish the Cleavage Binding

Depending on the depth of the cleavage, you may have a more or less pronounced flap of binding to sew down. The idea behind the previous step is that you don't want to add fabric into the cleavage; there will be plenty of fabric to turn the binding and a natural fold will appear.

If you aren't a fan of stitching folds closed on corners, it's critical that you do so on cleavage. As the quilt is manipulated, this fold can become undone and it will be challenging to get it refolded without partially deconstructing the binding.

With the binding laying flat against the front side of the quilt, open up the cleavage to reveal the seam allowance that covers the clipped seam allowance.

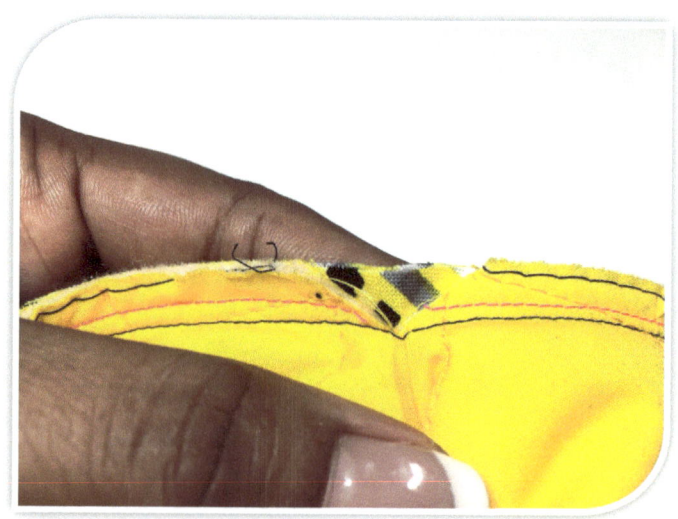

Using a sharp pair of scissors, cut away the bulk of the seam allowance. Be careful not to cut too close to the stitching so you don't create a hole at the edge of your quilt.

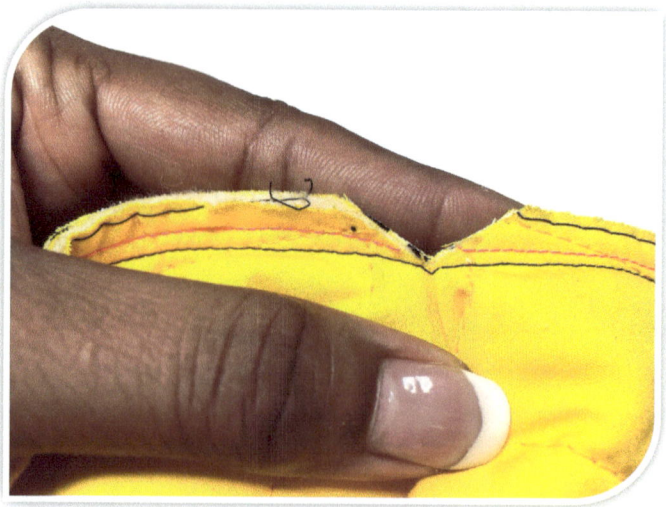

Part 8: Binding Cleavage

Lay the quilt flat on a table with the right side down, and the quilt in its natural position.

Pull the binding up through the cleavage and finger crease the binding so that it is evenly distributed through this gap.

Push the binding to one side, so the fold is laying flat along one side of the cleavage.

Insert a stiletto into the top of the fold, and fold it back on itself so you have the folds stacked and the center of the fold near the center point of the cleavage.

Binding Crazy Angles: Mastering Curves, Points, Cleavage, and More

Using one of the pins, pin the center point of the binding to the quilt, covering your stitching line.

On the right side of the cleavage, use binding clips to keep the binding flat in the cleavage as you work.

Fold down the left side to cover the stitches.

Use another binding clip to hold the left side in place. You can just see the bulk of the fold you made in the binding peeking out on this side.

Part 8: Binding Cleavage

Check the fold on the front side to make sure it is visually pleasing.

If it's not, you can use a stiletto to push the fabric and smooth the fold.

Use a pin, if desired, to hold this fold in place while you work on stitching the binding.

Behind the Scenes:
I have to admit, I drew a bit of a blank when trying to describe the inside point of a shape without getting too technical. Once "cleavage" popped into my head, I couldn't get it out!

Thread your hand sewing needle with matching thread, and use a blind stitch to secure the binding to the back of the quilt, removing clips as you go.

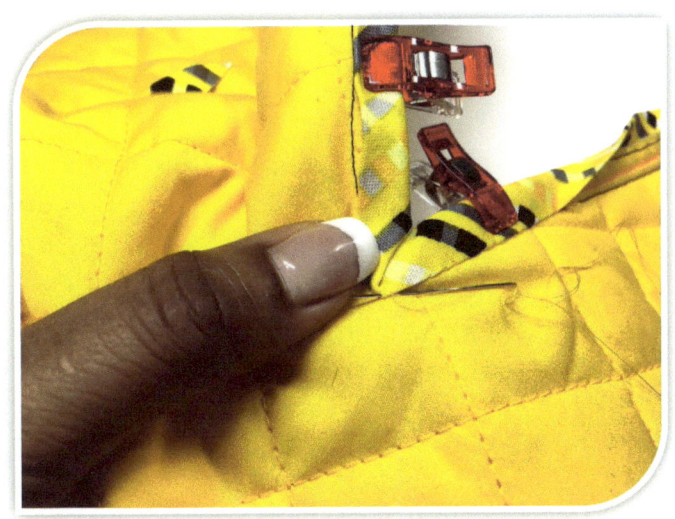

Binding Crazy Angles: Mastering Curves, Points, Cleavage, and More

When you get to the inside point, insert your needle into the bottom of the flap and take one or two stitches to secure it in place.

Stitch the flap down on the back and the front to keep it folded properly.

After stitching the flap, continue stitching along the binding until you come to the next corner.

If your next corner is different, see one of the earlier chapters for finishing that type of corner.

Part 8: Binding Cleavage

Your binding should be well-balanced on the front and the back, with a flat, pointed cleavage held securely with stitching.

Part 9: Finish the Binding

By this point, you've made it all the way around your quilt and you're ready to connect the ends of the binding.

I usually prefer to stitch the binding tails by machine, but what can make this challenging to do with crazy angles is that measuring the overlap can be undone by two factors: the stretch of the bias binding and whether the starting point was on a curve.

The technique shown here is a method that works well in situations where you don't have enough room along a straight edge to maneuver for machine stitching, as well as for bias binding situations that can distort the accuracy of the seam join.

If you're interested in learning the machine stitched join, check out the Resources chapter for further details.

Connect the Binding Tails

Lay your quilt on a flat surface, with the binding tails within reach. The starting binding tail should be flat on the quilt and the other, longer tail, loose.

The starting tail should be angled already with a ¼" hem pressed toward the inside of the binding.

Binding Crazy Angles: Mastering Curves, Points, Cleavage, and More

Gently smooth the binding tail and pin it to the quilt at the lowest point on the diagonal hem. If the end of your binding was angled the opposite way, this point might be facing down toward the quilt.

Insert the pin perpendicular to the edge of the quilt.

Overlap the loose tail over the starting binding tail. Using the Binding Tool, align the 1" measurement of the tool with the pin. Mark the lower edge using a chalk marker, directly onto the binding (blue arrow).

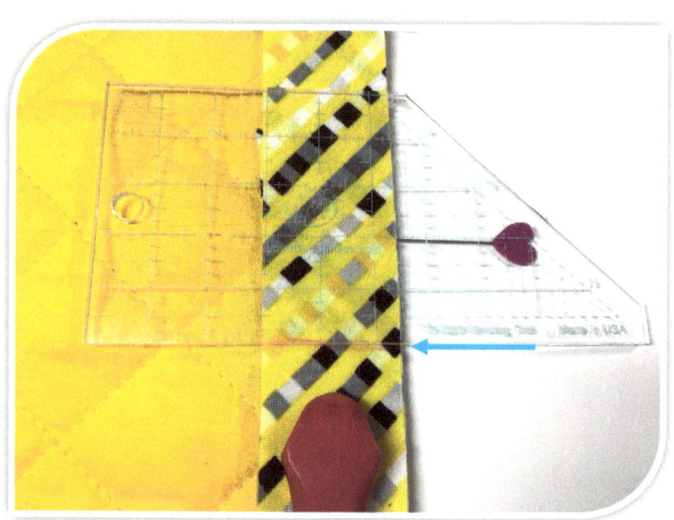

Part 9: Finish the Binding

Using a sharp pair of scissors, cut off the binding tail along the marked chalk line.

Open up the starting binding tail and insert the tail you just cut inside the binding.

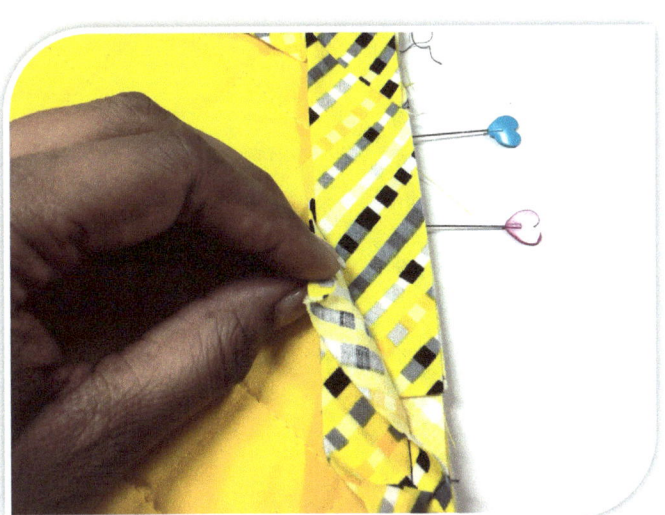

Feel free to use pins to help you secure the tails for sewing.

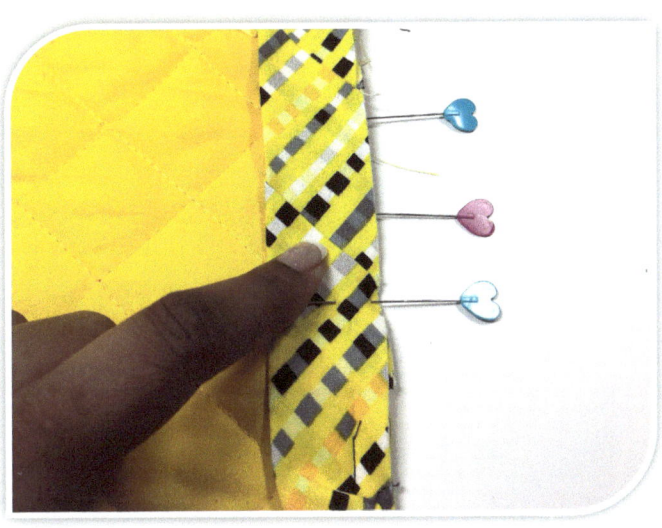

Binding Crazy Angles: Mastering Curves, Points, Cleavage, and More

Finish the Machine Stitching

Finish stitching the binding to the quilt.

After the seam is stitched, you will have an open fold where your tails overlapped.

Part 9: Finish the Binding

Use binding clips to fold over the binding to the back for hand stitching. This area is a little bulky, so the extra security provided by the clips is well worth it!

If you haven't done so already, fold and clip the binding to the remaining areas of the quilt, following the instructions for the corners as detailed in the previous chapters.

Stitch the binding to the quilt, using a blind stitch and covering the stitching line from the binding attachment.

As you work on the last section of binding where the tails overlap, don't forget to secure the open flap with hand stitches.

Now that I know how to successfully tackle these unusual corners, I have no problem adding unique finishes to any quilt.

I hope through this book, you also have developed confidence in your ability to finish quilts with crazy angles, and that you will not hesitate to work on projects with irregular edges.

> *I hope you've enjoyed learning these techniques, and I wish you many happy hours binding your quilts successfully, no matter what angles you encounter. Best of luck, and happy quilting!*

Part 10: Further Resources

There are so many things on the Internet, and so much more since I first conceived of this book years ago. I've tried to condense this to the best of the best, but nothing sits still on the Internet long enough to be immortalized in a book. I invite you to visit:

bindingcrazyangles.com

for updates, additional resources that couldn't be included here, plus interactive content. If you need working links for any of the products listed, you'll find those here too.

Where to Purchase

For the most part, I try to use commonly-available tools, but what's common in my sewing room and local shops isn't necessarily common everywhere!

I encourage you to shop your local independent retailer first, then your small online retailer (like me!), and as a last resort, try the big box, mass market retailers. When you shop small, and spend your money locally, you support your local community and keep our neighborhoods thriving!

LoveBug Studios – http://lovebugstudios.com

- Patchwork Pins and Binding Clips
- Hand Quilting Needles (Betweens)
- Binding Tool
- Aurifil Thread (some colors)
- Chalk Liner Pen (yellow only)

Doohikey Designs – https://doohikeydesigns.com/

- Binding Babies

For other supplies such as machine presser feet, please visit your local sewing machine retailer. Most machine manufacturers have a foot or accessory catalog that you can view on-line. Many of the major brands have versions of the recommended feet in their catalog.

Videos and Classes

Need to know how to block a quilt?

https://leahday.com/pages/how-to-block-a-quilt (Leah Day)

http://www.kimmyquilt.com/blocking-a-quilt.htm (Kimmy Brunner)

Want to learn how to add a scalloped border?

https://youtu.be/7Bm49sPpzu0 (Gourmet Quilter)

https://www.kristamoser.com/post/2017/06/10/cutting-scallop-borders (Krista Moser)

https://youtu.be/RQunyTO0-ZM (Laura Ann Coia)

Need an in-person or virtual class?

I travel around the country teaching this technique to hundreds of students a year, and will begin offering an on-line class on my website so I can reach more students. Check this link for upcoming in-person and virtual classes.

https://lovebugstudios.com/classes/binding-crazy-angles/

Part 10: Further Resources

Frequently Asked Questions

How do you choose thread to match the binding if the fabric is many colors?

First, I look to see if there's any single color that's dominating, or will appear more along the edge where I'll be stitching - like a background fabric.

If that doesn't work, I pick a color from the binding itself; something that blends, but doesn't stick out too much.

No matter what, I audition several colors by unspooling a few inches of several color choices and pick from there.

What's been really helpful for me is having enough variety of thread to choose from. In the beginning, I got a thread color card from Aurifil, and I would pick 2 or 3 spools of thread to try and order a small spool of each - the 200m spools are less than $5.

But it's kind of like fabric - you have tons of it and it's never the right color!

Over time, that's settled down quite a bit - I make a lot of quilts with similar colors.

I do try not to use monofilament; it's not good to use for both top and bobbin thread (the threads don't lock) so you still have to find a matching thread anyway.

Can you "bind crazy angles" by machine?

Yes, you can, but personally I haven't been as happy with the results. The miters are particularly challenging, and I sometimes find that I have to rip out sections to redo them.

Still, if you're interested in combining techniques, my book *Get It Done Now! Binding a Quilt by Machine* is available to purchase on my website.

Can I use a 40wt thread instead?

For attaching the binding, I would stick with 50wt, so you don't impact your seam allowance calculation and hide your hand stitches. It's your quilt though; do what you want!

Binding Crazy Angles: Mastering Curves, Points, Cleavage, and More

Can you use this technique for single-fold binding?

I don't normally do single-fold binding, but this is entirely possible, with a couple of modifications.

The math for calculating your binding width is going to be different; instead of (6) finished widths plus ease, you'll only need (4) binding widths plus ease.

When you stitch your binding to the quilt, you'll stop for corners, miter, and connect your ends in the same way.

When you turn your binding to the back, it's the same process you would use for hand stitching, however, you'll need to experiment with your ease measurement for the cut width of the binding. Ideally, you want to be able to fold the raw edge of the binding to touch the raw edge of the quilt, and then when you fold the binding to the back, the fold is just past your line of stitching.

What's the best and easiest way to make the corners even and flat?

Most people have problems with the corners of their binding because they aren't stopping in the right place, they aren't using a consistent seam allowance, or they don't fold their corner at the correct angle.

It's important to stop the same distance from any corner as the seam allowance you're using to stitch the binding to the quilt. That's what gives you a square corner. On crazy angles, you have to find this distance by measuring the seam allowance on the adjacent sides.

You can also have issues if you try to fold the miter in the opposite direction. This often makes people think their corner is too bulky so they have to clip it, when really the miter just has to be folded the other way.

I encourage you not to cut or de-bulk your corners other than what is called out in this book.

There's a section in each of chapters 5-8 that covers how to direct the bulk for each type of edge.

Part 10: Further Resources

BECOME A BINDING SUPERHERO!

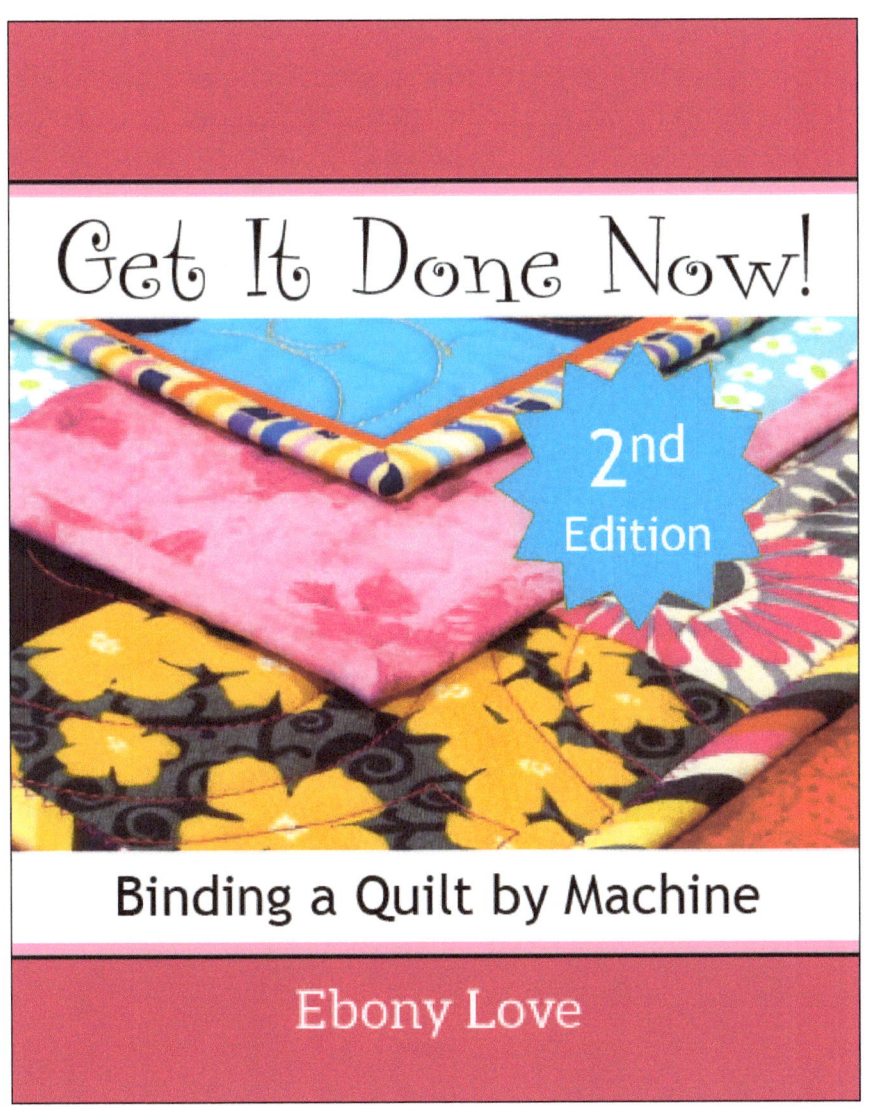

Also available from LoveBugStudios.com

Binding Crazy Angles: Mastering Curves, Points, Cleavage, and More

© 2019 Ebony Love. All rights reserved.

Binding Babies® is trademarked by Doohikey Designs® LLC. Use of this trademark in this book does not imply affiliation or endorsement of the contents by the trademark owner.

The book author retains sole copyright to the contributions to this book. No part of this book may be reproduced, stored in a retrieval system, or transmitted in any form, or by any means — electronic, mechanical, photocopying, recording, or otherwise — except for brief quotations for the purpose of review, without prior written permission of the copyright holder.

Every effort has been made to insure the accuracy of information in this publication; should you find any errors, please let us know at the address below and we will post corrections on our website.

Published by:

LoveBug Studios
1862 E. Belvidere Rd. PMB 388
Grayslake, IL 60030

http://lovebugstudios.com

ISBN 978-1-938889-15-8

Library of Congress Control Number 2019916322

Printed in the United States of America (US Distribution)

2 3 4 5 6 7 8 9 10

www.ingramcontent.com/pod-product-compliance
Lightning Source LLC
Chambersburg PA
CBHW042035150426
43201CB00002B/29